VE
YOUR
MEMORY
TODAY

IMPROVE YOUR MEMORY TODAY

ROB EASTAWAY
WITH
Dr HILARY JONES

ICON BOOKS

Published in the UK in 2009 by
Icon Books Ltd, The Old Dairy,
Brook Road, Thriplow,
Cambridge SG8 7RG
email: info@iconbooks.co.uk
www.iconbooks.co.uk

Previously published under the title
How to Remember:
a practical guide to memory recall
by Hodder & Stoughton in 2004.

Sold in the UK, Europe, South Africa and Asia
by Faber & Faber Ltd, 3 Queen Square,
London WC1N 3AU or their agents

Distributed in the UK, Europe, South Africa and Asia
by TBS Ltd, TBS Distribution Centre, Colchester Road
Frating Green, Colchester CO7 7DW

This edition published in Australia in 2008
by Allen & Unwin Pty Ltd,
PO Box 8500, 83 Alexander Street,
Crows Nest, NSW 2065

Distributed in Canada by
Penguin Books Canada,
90 Eglinton Avenue East, Suite 700,
Toronto, Ontario M4P 2YE

ISBN: 978-184831-064-3

Typesetting in Palatino by Hands Fotoset, Nottingham

Printed and bound in the UK by
CPI Mackays, Chatham ME5 8TD

Contents

Acknowledgements

I would like to thank all the people, too numerous to mention, who were prepared to talk to me so openly and honestly about their experiences with memory, and the many others who took part in my memory survey. You have helped to give this book a much more human touch. All the anecdotes in the book are true, though I have changed all the names to preserve anonymity.

I'm also indebted to Professor Tim Perfect at Plymouth University, who was able to fill in many of the blanks in the psychology of memory, and to point me in the direction of where else to look. Of the many books and papers on the subject, I would like to single out the work of Alan Baddeley (*Your Memory*) and Gary Small (*The Memory Bible*) as particularly valuable references.

Thank you Chris, Helen, Richard and Martin for your invaluable feedback on the early drafts; to Charlotte for setting it all up; and especially to Elaine and Jenna for all your comments and support, and for tolerating the many long evenings I spent in my office.

Preface

A good memory is something we very much take for granted, yet without it, we are lost. Impairment of memory is a perplexing and embarrassing disability that can impact severely on so many different aspects of our lives. When we cannot recollect even the most familiar constants in our regular routines our lives can become fractured and seriously socially handicapped. Most of us never have to give a second thought to where we left our house keys, what our telephone number is, or the names of our work colleagues, friends and relatives. We can state with confidence who the current prime minister is, what day of the week it is, and what we were planning to do at the weekend and with whom. But for many, and for a variety of different reasons, this simple, previously automatic recall becomes a jumbled and frustrating muddle. For them, it is easy to imagine that this is the inevitable beginning of some dire and terrifying degenerative process that will change their personality, alter their behaviour and ultimately threaten their sanity.

But happily, in most cases of simple forgetfulness there is a benign and innocuous explanation: a temporary lapse of concentration; a minor distraction; a period of stress. In most cases this faltering memory can be exercised, revived and rehabilitated much like an arthritic joint or an abdominal paunch.

Our memory is a vital and fascinating part of our minds, yet there remains so much about it which is medically unexplained and mysterious. We are astounded by stories of people who have extraordinary 'photographic' memories and who can apparently memorise entire telephone directories. We are amazed by those who retain outstanding and phenomenal memories for particular kinds of information, despite suffering from conditions such as autism or strokes. We are also drawn inexorably to newspaper stories of traumatic amnesia where a person suffering a blow to the head or waking from a coma has lost all recollection of their previous life and identity. It seems we really appreciate the bewildering power of our memory only when something goes wrong and interferes with it.

When problems do arise, whether they are minor or major, we know that any of the three main stages of memory can be disrupted. The first stage, registration of information, can easily be disturbed when the mind is distracted in someone who is stressed, anxious or depressed. Storage of information, the second stage of memory, can be upset by physical, hormonal or chemical imbalances in the brain. Recall, the third and final stage, can be jeopardised by degenerative processes, inflammation and ageing.

But of all of these potential causes of memory loss, perhaps the one underlying process we fear most is dementia, of which the commonest and most familiar type is senile dementia or Alzheimer's disease. Since up to 30 per cent of people over the age of 85 are affected by this, and since one of the earliest symptoms is that of gradual memory loss, our anxieties about this devastating condition are understandable. But the majority of us will never in fact suffer from dementia, and while a gradual and almost imperceptible loss of memory is a normal part of 'diminishing youth' (as I prefer to call growing older), there is much we can do to preserve our retention and recall of information so that we remain bright and alert in all our mental faculties right up until ripe old age.

Improve Your Memory Today explains how memory works, why it sometimes goes wrong, and what practical steps you can take to build a stronger memory, all while debunking some of the more popular myths about memory along the way. Drawing on the strategies and experiences of real people in their everyday lives, and with regular doses of gentle humour, this book takes a refreshing and supportive look at memory, how to understand and live with its defects and how to improve it. It includes details on why we forget, how anyone's memory can be improved, how to keep the brain active and healthy, tricks and strategies to help you remember, and much more.

I feel this will be of real practical benefit to many people throughout the UK, and I wholeheartedly commend it to anyone with any concerns whatsoever about becoming increasingly forgetful. So, if you remember nothing else today, at least remember this: this book is for you.

Dr Hilary Jones
London, 2009

Introduction

Margaret is worried about James' memory. Take yesterday, for example. The weather was chilly, there was ice on the windows, but despite reminding him about his scarf, Margaret watched James leave the room moments later without it, blissfully unaware of his almost instant memory lapse. One of these days, she says, he is going to catch his death of cold.

James is bad with names, too. When he has names to remember, James often forgets them within seconds or gets them hopelessly wrong.

And Margaret has noticed recently that James can't follow instructions at all. Unless she writes down exactly what he should do in a clear list for him to follow, he is bound to get muddled up somewhere.

Does James' experience sound familiar to you? Perhaps. But if you pictured James as somebody who is slowly losing his marbles, you were mistaken. James is nine years old. He may be a frustration to his mother Margaret, but James is a perfectly normal, healthy child, who happens, like most other children, to occasionally forget things. He forgets them because his mind is preoccupied with something else, or because the things he has to remember don't interest him. Does this worry him? Of course not.

So why tell this story? It's because forgetfulness is not a trait that belongs exclusively to people of more mature years. Forgetting is a normal and inevitable part of the way that the brain works at any age. Yet the older we get, the more anxious we are that imperfections in our memory are a sign of something more serious.

As you have chosen to read this book, you are probably at least curious about your own memory, and perhaps anxious about it and wondering if there is anything you can do. To which the answer is: yes, there are plenty of things you can do to improve your ability to remember things. You can also get a better understanding of how the brain works, which will reassure you that you are normal, and this in turn will reduce your *worry* about your memory. This last point is important, because one of the reasons why people forget things is because they are anxious. Anxiety about memory is therefore, to some extent, a self-fulfilling prophecy, but it can be overcome, partly by understanding more about what is going on when you remember and forget.

When most people think about memory improvement, they think of the techniques that are advertised in newspapers and magazines. Although these techniques are often accompanied by outlandish promises of how they will transform your life, they can be useful in certain circumstances, and you will find descriptions of some of them in the later chapters.

But there is more to memory improvement than a series of party tricks, fun though it may be to memorise a pack of cards in five minutes. Ask somebody what concerns them about their memory, and it might be something like 'Why am I forgetting names?' or 'Why do I forget why I came into this room?' It might be a general curiosity about whether it gets harder learn as you get older. Or it might be the anxiety expressed by one person I talked to recently, who asked bluntly: 'Will I end up like my parents?'

It is these general concerns about everyday memory that I wanted to deal with in this book. I'm not going to promise that 'You too will never again forget names or stories' because, as will become apparent as you read the book, my own memory is far from perfect. But you don't *need* to remember everything. This book will help you decide what you do need to remember, and what steps you can take to make your memory work better for you.

It is a practical book, and to help to make it so, I would encourage you to scribble in it, underline the parts that you think are important, and write notes. And if you are concerned about your memory, take comfort from the knowledge that you are not alone. Everyone forgets things now and then, but there's usually a way to help yourself, even if it's not as extreme as in the following story:

> *An elderly couple go round to their neighbour for dinner. After the meal, the two wives leave the table to go into the kitchen, while the husbands continue talking.*
>
> *'We're eating out a lot these days,' says one of the men. 'Just last night we went to a great new restaurant in town.'*
>
> *'Oh yes, which one?'*

'It was…' He pauses. 'You know, I think my memory's going. What's that flower with the thorns and the red petals?'

'A rose?'

'That's it!' he says, then shouts towards the kitchen. 'Hey, Rose, what was the name of that restaurant we went to last night?'

Part One:

The Background to Memory and Forgetting

1
Debunking the Myths

We all know something about memory. After all, we've been living with it all our lives. That doesn't stop us asking questions about it, and when this topic is discussed, there are some issues that seem to crop up time and again. In particular, people often ask if the following statements are true. What do you think?

1   Ability to remember gets worse with age.

    True/False

2   Adults typically use only about 10 per cent of their brain.   True/False

3   Alzheimer's disease is inherited from your parents.   True/False

4   Every important event that we experience is stored somewhere in the brain.   True/False

5   Men and women remember differently.

    True/False

6   Memory gets worse during pregnancy and never fully recovers.   True/False

7   Foods and supplements can boost your memory.   True/False

8   Memory techniques can permanently improve memory.   True/False

The world likes things to be simple. It is great to think that there is a definitive 'True' or 'False', black or white answer to each of the questions above. And in the spirit of keeping things simple, I will give you my true/false answers to each one in a moment.

However, let me start with a cautionary note. The world *isn't* that simple, particularly when it comes to the workings of the human brain. Much about human memory is now understood, but there is still plenty that is not.

Despite huge amounts of research conducted into memory by psychologists and neuroscientists, much of our understanding is still hazy, full of speculation and best guesses. Reputable research findings are peppered with phrases like 'There is evidence that …', 'In some cases it was found that …', 'Our theory is that …' and so on.

So, in answering the questions in the quiz at the start of this chapter, I have distilled the findings of the best scientific research to come up with my true/false answers. But as you will see, the scientific side of me won't allow me to give those answers without providing some of the background too.

Here, then, are the answers to the quiz.

1. Ability to remember gets worse with age.
Short Answer: TRUE

Let's face the facts. Memory relies largely on the cells in our brain, and as we get older, brain cells (neurons) die, and don't get replaced. The number of connections between the cells (synapses) also tends to diminish with age. The health profession hasn't yet found a way to reverse this trend.

In fact, we typically have 100 billion neurons at the age of eighteen, but then proceed to lose them every day thereafter. At its peak, daily cell loss may be 50,000 or more, though exactly how many neurons you lose on a given Tuesday in March, say, is unknowable. By the time we are 80, our brains are typically 10 per cent lighter, partly due to neurons dying, and partly due to them shrinking.

What this means is that, typically, a senior citizen will find it harder to absorb new information than a teenager, and will perform worse in tests that require rapid recall. In many social situations this will barely be noticeable. Other situations, such as quick-fire party games could almost have been designed to demonstrate the worst failings of aging minds. (No wonder grandparents often opt out of these games at Christmastime!)

So far, this all sounds pretty grim, but there are some important compensating factors. The average 50-year-old may perform worse in specific memory tests than the average student, but there are many who buck the trend. Fifty-year-olds can, and often do, have better memory powers than twenty-year-olds. Every individual is different.

Furthermore, there are some types of memory that typically *improve* with age. A 50-year-old may well be better at learning and retrieving historical or geographical information than a twenty-year-old. Why? Because the 50-year-old is likely to have more background knowledge about the subject, which makes it easier to place the new information in context.

Age also brings experience, which in turn can improve your ability to remember. Experience of how best to learn and how best to retrieve memories can help to compensate for having less processing power. In fact, an older adult trained in how to improve memory can easily outperform a younger adult who has not received such coaching in a memory test. And memory lapses, particularly so-called 'tip-of-the-tongue' moments (see page 55), are quite normal for all age groups, not just the elderly.

For the question 'Does the ability to remember get worse with age?', I prefer the fuller answer: Yes, *but experience compensates.*

2. The average adult uses only about 10 per cent of their brain.
Short answer: FALSE

The notion that we only use 10 per cent of our brains has entered popular folklore. This 'fact' is often used as the basis for showing how much potential there is for expanding your mind power in all sorts of different ways. It is a feel-good message that can be a good motivator for learning.

Depending on what source you read, we use only 10

per cent of our brains or as little as 1 per cent of our brains. The truth, however, is that nobody actually knows how much of our brain we use – though we can be certain that we don't use 100 per cent of our brains all the time because if we did, we would be trapped in an almighty epileptic seizure and unable to do anything at all.

So where did the 10 per cent myth come from? Nobody seems to be sure of its origin, though it may have entered popular consciousness when Albert Einstein allegedly told a reporter that he was only a genius because unlike most people he used more than 10 per cent of his brain. If the story is true, this was no more than a figure Einstein plucked out of the air to reflect the common-sense view that with a bit of effort, it's always possible to learn more.

Another possible source of the 10 per cent myth is the findings of various surgeons that the physical removal of small bits of the brain results in no discernible loss of memory or mental skill in some patients. One possible conclusion from this is that there are some parts of the brain that are redundant. Which parts, however, and just how much you can afford to remove before you start noticing the effects is not really known, though certainly if you were to remove 90 per cent of the brain, you would have, as Monty Python might have said, an ex-patient.

Modern brain scans have demonstrated that in a healthy person there are no 'inactive' parts of the brain. Different parts of the brain carry out different functions, and every corner is active at some stage during the day or night, whether it's to process a smell that has just been registered by the nostrils, to calculate a sum, or to co-ordinate the movements of the hand to stroke a dog.

However, the human brain has the capacity to perform some phenomenal feats, especially in the area of memory, more of which is discussed in Chapter 2. So, if the original statement had read: 'It is possible for most people, in the right surroundings and with the right method, to commit to memory ten times as things as they would otherwise have done' then the answer would be: TRUE.

3. Alzheimer's disease is inherited from our parents. Short answer: TRUE-ish (but other factors are more important)

The most extreme form of memory loss is associated with Alzheimer's disease. Sufferers of Alzheimer's progressively lose their memory and other cognitive functions. Diagnosing Alzheimer's disease is still an imperfect art. The best way of diagnosing it has always been in an autopsy. There are some distinctive neuron formations resembling tangles and plaques that always seem to found in the brains of acute sufferers. It is assumed, though not proven, that these tangles and plaques are linked to whatever it is that causes Alzheimer's, though it is also possible that they are simply a by-product of something quite different.

It is now known that there are many factors that affect our chances of developing the disease, of which our genes are one. There are certain rare gene variants that seem to be directly linked to early-onset Alzheimer's (that is, when the disease develops before the age of 60). However, less than 5 per cent of Alzheimer's cases belong to this category.

The most common gene that is known to be associated with Alzheimer's disease is a variety of what is known in shorthand as the APOE gene, and carriers of the APOE 4/4 gene (see 'The Most Common "Alzheimer" Gene' box) carry a greater risk of developing Alzheimer's in their 70s or early 80s.

The Most Common 'Alzheimer' Gene

APOE comes in three varieties: APOE-2, APOE-3 and APOE-4. (It looks like somebody forgot about APOE-1.) Everyone inherits one APOE gene from each parent, and the combination of these two inherited APOEs is known to have a significant influence on the chance of contracting Alzheimer's in one's 70s or 80s.

The two genes linked to Alzheimer's are APOE-3 and APOE-4, which you could think of as heads and tails on a very biased coin. If your parents have those genes, then you might end up inheriting one of three combinations:

- About 65 per cent of the population are born with APOE 3/3 , which is associated with a mild risk of late-onset Alzheimer's
- About 20 per cent have the APOE 3/4 combination, which roughly doubles the risk of developing Alzheimer's.
- About 2 per cent of the population have APOE 4/4. It is estimated that this combination increases your chance of developing Alzheimer's about tenfold compared to somebody who carries no APOE 4 gene.

The rest of the population carry at least one APOE 2 gene, and this is believed to offer some protection against Alzheimer's.

A carrier of APOE 4/4 might be at greater risk, but the important thing to note is that it doesn't make developing Alzheimer's a certainty. All sorts of other factors come into play, including for example general physical health, which seem to have at least as much influence as the gene. The idea that once you have a particular gene you will or will not develop Alzheimer's by a particular age is far from the truth. In fact, it is now believed that high blood pressure and cholesterol are both at least as significant in determining proneness to Alzheimer's as are APOE genes.

In fact, it may not be a question of if, but rather when.

Simply getting old is enough to increase the chances of Alzheimer's, from 2 per cent at the age of 70 to over 5 per cent at 80, and over 30 per cent for those aged 90-plus. Gary Small, a leading neuroscientist, has speculated that if we all live to the age of 110, almost everyone will acquire Alzheimer's.

This age factor is worth bearing in mind when you hear about people being tested for their proneness to Alzheimer's. While the presence of certain genes might bring it forward by a few years for some people, it seems that until a treatment is found, we are all destined for senile dementia in the end, from Alzheimer's or other disorders such as Parkinson's Disease – unless a bus or something else gets us first.

But there is good news. Knowledge about Alzheimer's disease is advancing rapidly, not least because the affluent and influential 'baby boom' generation are now getting to an age where they are beginning to worry about whether this awful condition will affect them. (When a rich, vocal group starts to make a noise, investment and research soon follow.) With this growing knowledge, we can expect breakthroughs in the treatment of Alzheimer's.

And even before these breakthroughs, scientists are confident that a combination of good diet, exercise and an active mind can do a lot to help delay its onset. So it's important not to develop a fatalistic attitude just because a parent has been a sufferer.

4. Every important event that we experience is stored somewhere in the brain.
Short answer: FALSE

In recent years, there have been many stories about the use of hypnosis to retrieve memories that had been suppressed, for example in the sensitive area of adults who were abused as children. This has revived the notion that *all* memories might be retrieved in this way.

What first prompted the idea that this claim *might* be true was the work of the neuroscientist Wilder Penfield in the 1950s. Penfield was trying to locate the parts of the brain responsible for epilepsy, by stimulating different areas of the brain with an electrical probe. In doing so he discovered that stimulating the temporal lobes – located on each side of the brain – often produced a spontaneous memory event. The patient would report an image they had seen or a sound they had heard, or occasionally would call out a snatch of a song, for example. When he probed in the same place again, exactly the same memory was reproduced. What was even more interesting was that sometimes the memories were ones that the patient could not recall in normal circumstances.

All of this led Penfield to speculate that memories are located at specific points in the brain, and that since the probes brought out memories that the patient couldn't otherwise recall, this was probably a sign that everything that is observed gets remembered. If only the path to those memories could be found, it would be possible to remember everything we had ever learned.

However, this was no more than speculation, and considerable doubt has since been cast on these findings. For one thing, many of the memories stimulated were meaningless mumbles or snatches, and in those cases where a coherent but unremembered memory was stimulated, it was impossible to say whether this was a real memory being retrieved or just a combination of familiar memories being temporarily wired together to form something apparently new.

There are billions of connections in the brain, and in theory there seems to be an almost limitless capacity to store information. But few researchers now believe that everything we experience and learn gets permanently hard-wired into the brain. More likely, as memories recede they become merged with other memories and in many cases disappear altogether. You will find more about the process of forgetting in Chapters 3 and 4.

5. Men and women remember differently.
Short answer: FALSE

There is a subtle distinction between whether men and women remember in different *ways*, and whether they remember different *things*. Of course men and women remember different things. Psychometric tests demonstrate this clearly enough, but it doesn't take a scientist to find convincing evidence. Women as a whole tend to pay attention to different things from men, thanks to both their genes and their upbringing, and their memories will therefore differ accordingly. Ask any mixed couple leaving a party to describe the people they met, and the woman will almost certainly recall separate facts from her partner. Among other things, the woman might remember more details about, say, what people were wearing, while the man will be more likely to remember the jokes. (This is not, of course, a hard and fast rule.)

It's common knowledge that the brains of men and women are different. For a start, there is the obvious physical difference that adult male brain is typically 10 per cent heavier than the adult female brain. However, the size of the human brain you are born with has little if any relation to intelligence or other cognitive abilities, as the superior performance of girls in many school subjects testifies. (Though as I mentioned before, your brain will shrink with age as neurons die off, and that *will* affect your cognitive abilities.)

However, men and women do have different aptitudes, which are partly a result of different wiring of the male and female brains. Men tend to be better at spatial awareness, and more of the male brain is devoted to this type of thinking. Women tend to perform better in language tests, and a larger region of the female brain is activated when dealing with language.

Whether it is the wiring of the brain or upbringing that causes men to be more interested in football tables and women to be more interested in fashion, the fact is that by being interested in those things they will study them more closely and will therefore remember them better.

So men and women remember different things. But that doesn't mean that they remember things *in different ways*. Individual people use a surprisingly varied range of methods for remembering, but there is not really a distinction between a 'male approach' and a 'female approach'. It depends much more on the individual's own style, regardless of gender. For this reason, I will make little distinction in the rest of this book between men and women when it comes to memory.

6. Memory gets worse during pregnancy and never fully recovers.
Short answer: FALSE (apart from the last stage of pregnancy)

I don't think I have ever met a mother who didn't believe that pregnancy had affected her memory. Surprisingly, though, scientific research in controlled conditions throws some doubt over the extent to which memory really does suffer during and after pregnancy.

In one study, a group of pregnant and non-pregnant women were given various tasks to perform including memorising lists of words and carrying out two tasks at once (divided attention such as listening to a recording while following a recipe). The overall performance of the two groups was the same. However, the pregnant group consistently *claimed* that their memory was worse than it had been before they were pregnant. The conclusion drawn was that the overwhelming changes that accompany pregnancy, including sleep deprivation, discomfort and the new responsibilities around the corner, lead to a mild attention deficit disorder. On top of this, the researcher suggested, there is a stereotype of the levels of memory loss expected at various stages of life, and women may be influenced by those stereotypes. All of this is pretty contentious stuff. However, other studies have found that there are definite hormonal and chemical changes in the brain during pregnancy, and that these same chemicals are known to play a part in memory formation.

So – as is the case with so many areas of psychology – there is no absolute certainty about memory loss and pregnancy. What does seem to be widely agreed is that memory is affected during the final three months of pregnancy, and that it generally returns to normal within at most a few months of the birth. Of course, once there is a baby around the house, the parents, and particularly the mother, are likely to have far more tasks to perform and things to remember, and all of this while being under stress. It would hardly be a surprise if there were more incidents of forgetting under these conditions, but this is more to do with the environment than any permanent decline in the brain's ability to function.

7. Foods, supplements and drugs can boost your memory.
Short answer: TRUE (but not much)

Scarcely a month goes by without a story about some

new food, supplement or drug that has been found to improve memory. What rarely makes it into the news story is the equally important statement of *how much* it improves the ability to remember, or indeed of what an improved memory actually means.

Food for Thought?

For a while in the 1960s there was a stir in the world of psychology when a scientist called James McConnell offered evidence that memory could be transferred by cannibalism. McConnell trained a group of flatworms to respond to light by curling up. The way he did this was to give them an electric shock every time they were exposed to light, to which they responded, quite understandably, by curling into a ball. Eventually, like Pavlov's dogs salivating at the sound of a bell, they would curl up when the light shone even though they were not being given a shock.

McConnell then chopped up the curling flatworms and fed them to their cannibalistic cousins who hadn't been trained to respond to the light. According to his report, the untrained flatworms now began to respond to light by curling up. It seemed as if memory had been directly transferred simply by eating – a notion worthy of science fiction, since it opened up the possibility that memory and knowledge might be acquired in the form of food. Eating books instead of reading them? Now there's an intriguing thought.

As it turned out, however, McConnell's results couldn't be reproduced by other scientists, and the notion of transferring memories by ingesting them died away. It is extremely unlikely that we will ever be able to implant information in the brain in the way that we can implant an encyclopaedia chip into a computer.

Food, supplements and drugs *can* measurably improve performance in various memory tests, such as recalling items on a list, but this improvement is usually only small, perhaps 5 to 10 per cent. These improvements are usually short-term, and are caused by two things:

- chemical changes in the brain, which make it more receptive to learning and forming memories or more alert to retrieve them;
- 'feel-good' effects, in which the very act of taking something that you think is doing you good makes you more relaxed and positive, and leads to improved performance.

Diet and drugs can also help memory in the long term. However, this is unlikely to be seen in the form of an improvement. What good diet and some drugs can do is help to maintain your memory at its current level, arresting the decline that might otherwise have happened. I discuss some of the drugs and foods recommended to help the memory processes in more detail in Chapter 6.

There is still hope that we might be able to restore, or at least massively boost, our memories by consuming a pill. Maybe, one day, it will happen. Though watch out – a pill that helps you to remember might also reduce your ability to forget, and as Chapter 3 explains, forgetting can be a good thing.

8. Memory techniques can permanently improve memory.
Short answer: TRUE

Memory books have been known to make ambitious claims for what their techniques can achieve. 'Never again will you struggle to remember names', claims one. For most people, these claims are unrealistic. Even with the best memory aids, the occasional memory lapse is inevitable for all but those few who have remarkably well-attuned minds. But just because memory aids cannot make memory *perfect* doesn't mean that they cannot *improve* memory.

Almost always, the aids referred to in books and courses are what might be called internal or mental aids for storing and retrieving memories – techniques like visualisation and mnemonics. However there are more familiar, external aids that we all use to some extent. These include diaries, knotted handkerchiefs, albums and of course that invaluable source of recollection, other people. ('Darling, can you remember where I left the keys?')

But how effective are the mental aids? Some

advertisements give a misleading impression that there is somehow 'a technique' that will boost your memory for everything. This is most definitely not the case. A technique that might help you to remember an important date is unlikely to help you to remember to post a letter or to remember what you did yesterday. As we'll see later, memory takes many different forms, and different aids help to remember different things. Some aids are there to help you to form short-term memories, such as a taking a phone number when you don't have a pen to hand, while others are aimed at helping to form long-term memories of important information.

In general, if you take two random groups of people, and train one group in memory techniques and make sure that the trained group continues to apply their learning, then the trained group will significantly outperform the untrained group in memory tests. The theory is that these improvements also apply in everyday situations, though the results are much harder to measure in those circumstances.

About half of the people I surveyed have consciously applied techniques they have learned to help their memory in everyday activities. Some had either found the techniques didn't really work for them, or had proved to be too much bother. However, many people do find these techniques to be a genuine help.

I can personally vouch for the number memorising scheme I describe on page 153, which I have used over two decades. Though it isn't foolproof, I can think of several occasions where I have remembered a number

I would otherwise have forgotten. This technique has therefore made a permanent improvement to my ability to remember numbers. However, that improvement has not been without effort, and it still requires perhaps ten seconds of concentration for the process to work. I have friends who either see no need for such a technique, or see it as too much hassle.

So, while there is no magic cure, no instant fix that will sort out your memory problems for ever, there is no question that you can successfully and measurably improve your memory in areas where you want to do so, as long as you are committed .

How did you do with the True or False test? Maybe one or two myths have been debunked for you.

Here are some of the important conclusions.

For both men and women, memory does generally weaken with age, and some memories do get lost forever. But although we don't have vast untapped areas of the brain to develop, we can improve our general memory through wisdom and experience, can use memory techniques to help out in specific areas, and can even get a small benefit from supplements and drugs. With Alzheimer's and other forms of dementia there is a genetic factor that we may be lumbered with, but diet, exercise and attitude are big factors in keeping it at bay.

2
Brains and Computers

Topics covered

- The astonishing powers of human memory
- How brains and computers differ

'I've got a lousy memory.'

How often have you found yourself saying something like that? You are most likely to say it just after suffering some annoying lapse when trying to retrieve a familiar piece of information.

However, memory is far more than retrieving facts. It is also the ability to process and file information in the first place. It is the ability to remember language and names, what you did and when, what you learned, how to do things (such as tying a shoelace), what you are going to do in the future, what things taste, sound and look like ... and much more.

The truth is that when you look at the bigger picture of what memory is, most people are endowed with quite phenomenal abilities. Children and adults are all capable of feats that no computer could rival.

The astonishing powers of human memory

It's easy to take for granted just how astonishingly powerful the memory is of even an 'average' person.

Every second of every day, your senses are bombarded with information. It is the job of your brain to store and retrieve all of the vital information that it needs, in order to give you the best hope of survival. How would a computer go about doing this? It would have little choice but to store every bit of data that it received, while at the same time checking to see whether something just experienced linked back to an important related item in its memory bank. The processing and storage power required would be huge, and after a few hours at most, even the most powerful home computer would be screaming, 'Enough, enough!' (or computer-speak to that effect). You just have to think how much space a short video clip on your computer takes up to realise how memory-hungry audiovisual information can be. And that is ignoring the other senses of smell, touch and taste that your typical desktop is currently incapable of detecting.

Your brain, however, can cope easily with this deluge of information. For example, think of yourself walking down the street. As you take a leisurely stroll, your brain is hard at work. As you look around you, your brain picks up the scan of all the faces of the people you see and compares them with the faces of all the people you have ever met to see if you recognise any of them. It does this in an instant. Think about the last time you bumped into somebody you recognised. It probably took you less than a second to register not only that you knew them, but also some of the key information about how you knew them.

A blink of an eye later, your brain is checking to see if there are any new items on sale in the window of a shop. It can recognise what is new only because it managed to effortlessly remember what items you saw in that same shop window last time you went past (as opposed to the time before, or the time before that).

Meanwhile, you are carrying in your head a shopping list, while also carrying information about what you have in the house and what condition it is in, so that if you spot a bottle of washing-up liquid you can decide to purchase it because you remember that the bottle at home is almost empty. And all of the time you are carrying a mental map of which route you will take around the various places you want to visit, while at the same time scanning the roads to check that the cars or other pedestrians aren't doing anything abnormal that might endanger you as you make your way.

This scale of multitask processing would be too much for all but the most powerful of computers. And unlike a computer, you can continue to do this day after day without any risk of your brain ever becoming 'full'.

In the light of this, accusing memory of being lousy seems not only misguided, but positively ungrateful.

How brains and computers differ

It is natural that we make comparisons between human memory and that of a computer. The more that computers become a part of our everyday lives, the easier it is to draw analogies between the way that we store and retrieve information and the way that our machines do.

A colleague of mine who has not been averse to the odd pint of beer or five in his time, uses such an analogy all the time when referring to his memory. 'My processor is OK,' he says, 'but I've got a corrupted hard disk.'

On one level, there are many similarities. A human's short-term memory is a bit like a computer's RAM – temporary information that helps you to tackle a problem, but which isn't needed in the long term and so isn't saved. As my friend suggests, long-term memory serves as your hard disk. And CDs and USB sticks – information that can be stored separately from the computer – have their parallels in the photo albums and other memorabilia that we keep around the house.

However, when it comes to understanding the strengths and weaknesses of the human brain, it's important to recognise the many ways in which it differs from a computer. Table 1 shows some other differences between a computer and a brain.

Table I: Differences between a computer and a brain

COMPUTER	HUMAN BRAIN
Computer hard disks become full.	Brains never become full, as far as we know, though there may be some subtle

Computer	Human Brain
	merging and 'overwriting' of old information.
Computers don't forget unless told to do so ... which is one reason why they fill up.	Forgetting is a fundamental part of the way the human brain efficiently holds onto only its most important information.
Computers store and retrieve information literally ... which means, of course, garbage in, garbage out.	Humans store information by comparing it to what they have seen before, often 'adapting' the information to fit stereotypes so that only the essential elements are retained.
Computer memories typically allocate a fixed amount of space for each specific function (though this has begun to change).	The brain tends to adapt depending on what it is used for. If you become a crossword addict, the area of your brain devoted to language expands of its own accord ('Use it or lose it', as they say).
Memory of a specific item, such as a name, is stored in a single location.	One item may be stored in numerous places.

Computer	Human Brain
One small fault in the hard disk can make a whole set of data irretrievable.	This is where the human brain comes into its own. Because memories typically have a series of associations, losing one of those links (because of a stroke, say) doesn't mean the memory is necessarily lost – the brain simply has to discover a different route to the same information.
The ability of a computer to retrieve information is not affected by its surroundings.	Human memory (both storing and retrieving) is enormously influenced by surroundings. Just walking into a room can trigger a flood of memories that were formed when you were previously in that location.
The transfer of information from the computer's working memory (the screen, say) to its permanent store (the hard disk) is clear-cut. Press save, and it's done.	The transfer of information from short-term working memory to long-term 'hard-wired' memory in humans is usually a gradual process, often requiring several exposures before something is permanently set.

Many of the differences are in the brain's favour – it is an incredibly powerful organ, and as I mentioned earlier, the brain enables you to plan, to remember and to react to events over a lifetime in a way that no current computer could manage even for a day.

Understanding these differences is a key to understanding how we can boost our own memory's performance. In the next chapter, I'll look at some of these differences in more detail.

3
How the Brain Remembers

Topics covered

- Remembering by association
- Taking short-cuts to make things simple
- The impact of emotions
- Forgetfulness or absent-mindedness?
- Why forgetting is important

Remembering by association

One of the most important features of human memory is that while computers store information in hierarchies, the brain stores information through an intricate web of associations.

Imagine you want to store information about somebody called Mike Howells, who lives at 90 Larkin Road. A computer would file this in a structured database. It would open the file labelled 'contacts', run through the surnames until it found the right place in the alphabetic listing to file 'Howells', go to the fields labelled 'name' and 'address', and then enter the data. Retrieving the information would take a similarly rigid route.

The brain's method of storing information is far less direct. In storing Mike Howells at 90 Larkin Road, you are likely to make all sorts of conscious or subconscious links to embed this in with your other memories. No two people would memorise this address the same way, but here is how I think I would do it, to demonstrate the apparently chaotic series of links that are created when forming a memory:

> *Howells was the name of a dentist I once knew …*
> *90 … one of those numbers quite near 100 … 90 was*
> *the start of a decade…the year when I first went*
> *freelance … Larkin was the name of that family in*
> *the TV series with David Jason … also a poet … it's*
> *Larkin Road so I picture it as quite a busy place,*
> *unlike an avenue or a lane …*

Such memories are normally recorded in our brains with little effort, and while it might sound like I was using a deliberate memory technique to store that information, as far as I can tell that is the 'natural' way that I responded to Mike Howells' address. It's unlikely that you would make the same associations as I did, and you might not even be conscious of how you absorbed the information, but I suspect that you experienced a similar process to mine.

When it comes to *retrieving* the memory of where Mike lives, the process of associations operates in reverse. To give myself a chance to observe this process, I'm now going to leave the word-processor, have my lunch, allow the memory of Mike's address to disappear from my working memory, and then come back and see if I can trace the way that I recall Mike's details. See you shortly …

... OK, I'm back, and desperately trying not to look at the previous paragraph. Actually, Mike's full details have come back to me quite rapidly – it seemed to take only a second or so – but I'll reproduce roughly what seemed to happen.

> *Mike's surname is Howells – I knew a dentist called Howells once – address ... I'm picturing David Jason in a bath ... Pa Larkin ... it's not Larkin Drive or Avenue, it's more normal sounding than that ... Larkin Road sounds right ... the number 9 comes to mind, except it's a bigger number ... 90 ... and I know it's 90 because I remember thinking that was the year when I first started working for myself ... so it's 90 Larkin Road.*

Now I think about it, I believe I can actually picture '90 Larkin Road' and where it appeared on the page, almost like a dim photographic memory, so I'd know roughly which corner of the book to look in if I needed to remind myself. Perhaps you have had the same experience when looking up something in a book you read recently?

That little demonstration indicates just how 'rich' the process of recall can be, based on a combination of trial and error to see which routes create familiar associations, and all sorts of visual and other cues that point in the right direction. Sometimes recall is instantaneous; at other times you can almost feel yourself wandering through a maze, getting warmer and warmer until the fact emerges. This is all very different from the direct and structured way in which a computer retrieves information.

Game, Set and a Perfect Match

In the middle of writing this chapter, I happened to have an appointment at the local barber's. My hair was cut by Maria, an Italian who is a tennis fanatic, and our conversation turned to famous tennis matches. 'Do you remember that great final between Borg and McEnroe?' she asked. 'It was on the same day as my brother got married because we watched the match after the ceremony. When was it? It must have been 4 July, Independence Day, because we always joked to my brother that his wedding was the day he lost his independence! It was the same year Charles and Diana got married, whenever that was.'

When I got home, I checked on these facts and they were all spot on – Borg v. McEnroe, Wimbledon final 4 July 1981, a few weeks before Charles and Di's wedding. Maria's rich set of associations between Independence Day, her brother's wedding, Charles and Diana and the tennis have helped her to accurately store this memory. Furthermore, she could use this information in lots of ways; for example to remember the day of that tennis match (same day as her brother's wedding) or to remember her brother's wedding (same day as that tennis match!).

Taking short-cuts to make things simple

One reason why computers can be so inefficient at storing information is that they usually store literally everything they are presented with, whether it is important or not. The brain, however, takes short-cuts. In Table 1, which compared computers and brains, I mentioned that brains often fit what they are fed into familiar patterns or stereotypes. After all, if you see a picture of a concrete office-block, why bother to record the details of the window dimensions when broadly speaking it looks like all the other concrete office blocks you have seen. What you will remember is a broad impression of an office-block (maybe even one you saw on another occasion), rather than a photograph of this particular one. Unless, that is, you make a particular effort to commit this one to memory.

Our natural tendency to fit what we see into familiar patterns can have some amusing side effects. It means that we sometimes register what we want or expect to see, rather than what we actually see. What we observe and what we *think* we observe are often two different things.

PARIS
IN THE
THE SPRING

Your eyes just passed over a triangle containing some words. Without looking, can you say what the words in this triangle were?

If what you read was 'Paris in the spring', you are not alone, though what it actually says is 'Paris in *the the* spring'. This little perception trick shows how the brain will often register what it expects to see rather than what it does see. 'Paris in the spring' is a familiar phrase already locked in the memory, and by calling on that familiar memory the brain saves the effort of having to re-interpret what it sees.

If the triangle had said:

… then, although the pattern of words is the same as before, you have probably read it correctly into your working memory, with a double '*deb*', because the pattern is unfamiliar, and therefore worthy of the extra attention.

The impact of emotions

Emotions are an important factor in the formation of memory. Whether it is love, shock, laughter or fear, heightened emotions significantly increase the chance of something registering in the brain. There is a particular part of the brain known as the amygdala that becomes more activated when emotions are aroused.

Because our memories are tied to feelings, we can sometimes remember more about how an event *felt* than what actually happened. So, for example, you can remember that you felt angry or exhilarated but can't remember what was said.

In some circumstances the emotional impact can actually distort the memory itself. Even the use of emotive words can influence the formation of a memory.

In one of the most notable experiments to test the reliability of witnesses, psychologist Elizabeth Loftus showed a video of a two cars running into each other. She divided the audience into two groups. She asked the first group to estimate how fast the cars were going when they *contacted* each other. The average speed estimated by the group was 32 mph. She then asked the second group to estimate how fast the cars were going when they *smashed* into each other. The estimated speed rose to an average of 41mph, despite the fact that they had witnessed the same event.

The simple use of the word 'smashed' instead of 'contacted' suggested to the audience that the event had been more dramatic. This change of wording significantly influenced the witnesses' memory of the event: when the groups were then asked if they saw any broken glass on the road, the 'contacted' group said, 'No'; the 'smashed' group said, 'Yes'. (In fact there was no glass.) What is worrying is that this demonstrates that in a court of law, leading questions could actually cause the witness to innocently change their evidence, and become convinced that they remember something that didn't actually happen.

Forgetfulness or absent-mindedness?

Our ability to focus on the details that interest us to the detriment of other inputs can lead to another quirky feature in the human brain.

There is a delightful experiment, based on studies first done by psychologists back in the 1970s, that has become increasingly famous in the last couple of years. In the experiment an audience is invited to watch a video of a group of people playing basketball, and to count how many times the team dressed in white bounce the ball. The film clip, which is viewable via YouTube, lasts about 30 seconds, and after about ten seconds, while the basketball players are busy passing the ball to each other, somebody dressed in a gorilla suit walks into the middle of the playing area, waves at the camera, and walks off. (A similar idea, involving a moonwalking bear, was used in an awareness campaign for road safety.)

At the end of the video, the group are asked how many times the ball was bounced, and whether they noticed anything unusual. The group invariably gets the count almost exactly right, but amazingly most people fail to notice the gorilla. When I first saw this,

I was one of about 90 out of 100 in the audience who had noticed nothing odd in the video. When we watched the film again, it was hard to believe we hadn't spotted such an obvious intervention.

This demonstrates as clearly as anything how the brain is able to focus so much on one area of interest that it can completely ignore information that it deems to be irrelevant to the task. This phenomenon has even gained a technical description: it is known as *inattentional blindness*. We can be literally blind to things that we are not concentrating on.

This helps to explain another reason why the brain is so efficient – it doesn't waste effort storing everything that the eyes see and the ears hear, but selects the things that it believes are important. However, this strength can also appear to be a weakness.

We often blame memory when the real culprit is *absent-mindedness*, something we associate not with people whose brains are failing but with people who are close to genius, the so-called 'absent-minded' professor. In fact absent-mindedness can afflict anybody. It comes from the mind concentrating so much on one matter that it completely closes off its attention to other functions and performs them on autopilot

This might account for many occasions where people have a complete aberration, such as walking into a room and forgetting why on earth they went in there in the first place. In similar vein, I remember a moment aged about fourteen when I'd just had a shower, had a shirt in my hand and reached for a tissue to wipe my nose. Busy thinking about some important matter, I then tossed the shirt into the bin. If that happened to me now, I might get seriously worried at the decline in my faculties, so it's nice to have the reassurance of having done something so ludicrously absent-minded at such an early age.

One other positive thing is that while memory failure is generally deemed to be a negative thing, absent-mindedness has quaintly positive connotations. So if it helps, when in doubt call it absent-mindedness, not memory loss.

Learn to recognise those moments when absent-mindedness has made you forget something, and think about ways to improve your concentration rather than worrying that your memory is failing

Why forgetting is important

What we blame our memory for more than anything is, of course, forgetting. In the next chapter, I'll look into how and why we forget, but before that let's look at the benefits of forgetting.

One benefit of forgetting that I've already mentioned is that it helps to remove unnecessary clutter from our minds. If I go shopping at the supermarket, it's helpful to remember what is on my shopping list. But this list is not of much use when I visit the supermarket next time. Clearly I have a need to remember this list for perhaps a few hours, after which it is redundant. The brain is remarkably good at 'knowing' how to forget information that it no longer needs – information like old shopping lists, your schedule for the previous week, the seating arrangement for last night's dinner party. All of this was important to know at the time, but would become inconvenient clutter if you retained it for very long.

It is hard to know which would be worse – never being able to remember, or never being able to forget. Both would be grim, but I suspect that the extreme forgetful state is not as bad for the sufferer as it is for those caring for him. People with acute memory loss can sometimes live in quite a contented world, albeit one which resembles a scratched record that endlessly repeats itself.

On the other hand, never forgetting while others do forget could drive you to insanity. I'm reminded of the film *Groundhog Day*, and a less well-known, much darker film that inspired it, called *12:01 P.M.* In the latter, the central character Myron discovers that he is trapped in a world which progresses for exactly one hour, and then at 1pm it loops back to 12:01 and starts again. Unfortunately for Myron, his memory does not erase the previous hour, so he sees the same routine repeating itself again and again, with nobody able to share his experience. Needless to say, this experience becomes a living hell. (It's a great little film, by the way, I heartily recommend it!)

Forgetting is a gradual process that follows a surprisingly predictable path. If you commit to memory a batch of information and are later asked to recall it, as much as half of it might disappear in the first few minutes, two thirds in the first few hours, and maybe 90 per cent over the next few days, but the rate at which items are forgotten will slow down. Some memories will stick for many years, for no apparent reason.

This smooth decaying curve of forgetting seems to apply consistently across all age groups – the further back in time that you were exposed to something, the more likely you are to forget it. This might seem obvious, but this rule only applies to information that you do not recall in the interim. If you remembered somebody's name a year ago, and then were reminded of it only one week ago, that memory now counts as being only a week old, not a year old. So the fact that you remember things from your childhood is not simply down to the fact that it was an unforgettable time in your life, but also because you have relived those moments many times, keeping them 'fresh' in your mind. Those things that happened to you when you were six and to which you never gave another thought are likely to be irretrievably lost from your mind.

You could almost call this a 'natural selection' of memories. Those memories that you recall frequently are likely to be the ones that are important to you, and have relevance to your life today. These are the memories that are most likely to stick. Those memories that you don't recall are probably those that you don't need to remember, or don't want to remember (either because they aren't of particular interest to you or because they are unpleasant). These are the memories that will gradually be eroded away.

Women who have given birth are notoriously good at forgetting how painful the process was. The ability to forget pain is as powerful a reason as any for why it is good to have a brain that forgets.

S – The Man Who Couldn't Forget

There have been some famous cases of people who were unable to forget, and whose lives became miserable as a result. The most famous case of someone with an almost indelible memory was that of a Russian called Shereshevsky – an oddly difficult name to remember, which is why he is generally referred to in the literature as 'S'.

S was born with a condition known as synaesthesia, in which the stimulation of one of the senses produces a response in the others. When people with this condition hear a noise, it can create vivid images and even smells in their mind, and this multi-sensory condition makes everything they experience much more memorable.

When S was asked to memorise a word, he would not only hear it, but he would also see a colour and sometimes experience a taste in his mouth too. Partly because of the vivid memories that he created, he was able to remember the finest detail of things he'd been told ten or even twenty years earlier. Meaningless algebraic formulae, lists of names and poems in foreign languages would all stick. This became a problem for him, particularly when he decided to exploit his unique skills to become a stage memory-man. He became aware that he was still remembering information given to him by audiences in all his previous performances. He had to consciously learn how to forget, which he achieved, bizarrely, by mentally 'covering up' the images of things in his memory with a black cloth!

4
Why We Forget When We Don't Want To

Topics covered

- How forgetting happens
- Losing cells and connections
- Memory interference
- Faulty replication
- Deliberate memory distortion
- Tip-of-the-tongue syndrome

How forgetting happens

Forgetting may be a natural part of how the brain works, but not all forgetting is beneficial. It's frustrating not being able to remember all those things that you actually *do* want to remember, such as birthdays, names, directions and even where we parked the car at the supermarket. So why is it that, against our better wishes, we begin to forget even the useful stuff?

Errors in our memory can arise for three main reasons. To use the crude analogy of a video recorder, the problem might be:

- a faulty RECORD button;
- somebody messing with the tape by blanking out part of it, or changing the order;
- a faulty PLAY button.

Failing to store information (the faulty RECORD button) is largely down to the failure to concentrate sufficiently on the information and the failure to build enough associations to form the memory.

You can only *forget* something if you have stored it in the first place, so in this chapter we'll look at why the two other parts of the process of remembering go wrong – damage to what has been recorded, and problems playing it back.

If You Think Your Story is Embarrassing ... Part 1, The Abandoned Daughter

Jennifer and Bob were on a day trip with their adult daughter, Carol, and stopped off to get some petrol. While Bob filled up the car, Carol popped into the ladies' to pay a call. When Carol returned to the forecourt, she looked around and realised to her horror that her parents' car was no longer there. In fact, as it turned out, her parents had driven off without her, having *both* quite forgotten that their daughter was with them. The garage was out in the country, with no public transport, and it wasn't until four hours later that Carol's parents sheepishly returned to pick her up. To make matters even worse, the local newspaper got wind of the story and published it. Everyone found it hilarious except, of course, the family concerned.

Losing cells and connections

The most fundamental reason for the decline in memory is the slow deterioration in our brain cells that is an inevitable part of aging. Memories are stored through a complex network of interconnected neurons throughout the brain, and if the particular cells that store a memory are damaged or die then that's it, the memory is lost. Brain cells die naturally with age, though all sorts of things can speed up their disappearance, from physical blows like the thump when heading a football to the toxic effects of a glass of wine.

Normally, a memory is not an isolated , single piece of information stored in a single cell. Instead, it is formed from a whole series of associations to other memories, so that when recalling that memory, there might be several different 'paths' that could be taken to reach it. Even if the memory is still there, if the path to it is cut, then the memory is not retrievable and is therefore forgotten.

In the previous chapter, I gave you the address details of somebody called Mike Howells. Can you remember what that address was? More to the point, as you think about it, can you track *what route* you take to recall the information?

Maybe you will take the same route that I described when I was memorising it. I picture David Jason in a TV episode where he is playing Larkin … Larkin 'lots of traffic' … Road … year of 90 … 90 Larkin Road.

However, there are other ways that I might have got there. I associate certain sounds with the address, probably because I said it out loud when I first wrote it. For some reason I associate a sort of 'La la' sound with the address, which leads to 'La – kin', which then triggers 'Road', and for the number I can also sense that it's a nice round number that is quite close to 100 … 90 feels right.

Let's suppose that the brain cells with the vital link of the image of Pa Larkin now disappear from my brain. Fortunately, I still have an alternative route for getting to the address (the 'La la' route) so while it might take me a moment longer to track down this less familiar route, the memory of the address is still accessible.

If all of the cells that link through to the memory cease to function, then that memory is no longer accessible. The fewer 'alternative routes' there are for each memory, the more vulnerable that memory is to being lost by the random decay of the brain cells that access it. There's an important lesson here, that applies as much to a brain as it does to a computer, and that we'll come back to later when looking at ways of keeping your memory fit. The lesson is: *it always helps to have a backup, just in case*.

If You Think Your Story is Embarrassing ... Part 2, Wrong Day, Wrong Room

Hannah is a lecturer. She gives regular classes on medieval history, often (though not always) in Lecture Room 4 in her faculty building. One morning Hannah turned up to Room 4 a bit earlier than normal. To her surprise, the students were already there. Hannah expressed her delight at their keenness, and immediately launched into her class. Then one of her students piped up: 'Er ... Dr Philips, actually this isn't your lecture.' It turned out that not only was she in the wrong room on the wrong day, but there was already a lecture underway. Hannah had mistaken the lecturer for one of her students. Ouch!

Memory interference

Memories don't just disappear; they can sometimes become distorted over time. One way in which this happens is that memories can interfere with each other. Interference typically happens when there are two memories that are similar to each other and become bundled together. As memories recede into the past, the brain gets increasingly confused about whether two events happened on the same day as each other or at different occasions. For example, memories of two holidays that you spent in the same place are likely to become merged as they recede into the past. This is quite understandable given that there is no great evolutionary advantage to remembering exactly what happened when and where, but it is still exasperating if you are attempting to reminisce about those two different trips to Cornwall ten and fifteen years ago.

Interference can also lead to some memories overriding others. Most common is when the more recent memory obscures something similar that you learned earlier – for example today's shopping list will obscure yesterday's, and today's top ten in the music charts will obscure those from last week. This kind of interference, in which new memories tend to displace old ones, is known as *retroactive* interference. By and large it is a helpful part of forgetting, in that the new information is likely to be of more relevance than the old. It can have its downside, however.

Sports fans wanting to reconstruct in their minds the team that played the season before last will find themselves bringing together players who never actually coincided in a match. And in that party game where you go around the room creating a list of items to take on holiday, adding one each time, retroactive interference means that the item you heard most recently is likely to stick, but those that precede it are more likely to become jumbled or to disappear altogether, especially if they were similar items. For example 'hamster' will interfere with 'mouse' more than it will interfere with 'tractor', since the cues for hamster and mouse are very similar (small furry pet, lives in a cage …).

It isn't always the most recent memories that dominate. Sometimes the older memories are the ones that prevail in the long run, and this becomes an increasingly familiar experience as you get older.

I observe it particularly when I am trying to think of the sponsor of a big sporting event. I first watched the London Marathon in 1984 when it was sponsored by Mars confectionery. Since then it has been sponsored by ADT and Nutrasweet, and later by Flora, yet when I try to think of who the sponsor is now, I'm more likely to think of 'Mars' than of the other more recent sponsors. I have similar problems with naming the sponsors of football's League Cup, or of sponsored TV programmes such as *Who Wants to be a Millionaire?* The same tendency can apply to remembering anything from songs to who does what in the government; it will often be the older memories that dominate rather than the recent ones.

This phenomenon was first observed by a psychologist in the nineteenth century. Jost's Law, as it is known, says that if two memories have equal strength at a particular time, the older memory is the one that will last.

One way to demonstrate what is going on is to illustrate it with a graph. I have used the example of famous pop stars. When a new pop star emerges, they get instant, huge celebrity, and will tend to dominate the list of famous pop stars recalled by any fan.

I've imagined a pop fan called Jill who was in her teens when Robbie Williams became a star. When he first appeared, he was the top of her recall list. After a short period where he was the main focus of her attention, her memory of him began to decay (as all memories do). Then in 2002 Gareth Gates became a star. For several months he was the first pop star to be recalled by Jill. As the initial impact of Gareth Gates wore off and his memory faded too, the earlier memory of Robbie Williams regained dominance.

You can see in Diagram 1 how the two graphs of Gates and Williams actually cross over. Before Gareth Gates came along, Robbie Williams was the only one of the pair to be recalled (of course!). Then when Gates

Diagram 1: Jost's Law: How older memories can dominate in the long run

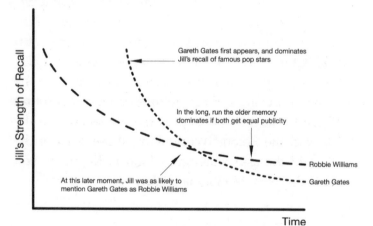

arrived, he was the first name to be recalled, though his dominance immediately began to decay, until his graph dipped below that of Williams. If the two were to continue to get a similar level of exposure to each other, it is Williams who would be the most memorable to Jill in the long term, because he was the earlier memory and had greater impact to start with.

All things being equal, it is the first of a kind that will make the biggest impact, so the pop stars from your teens will have more impact on you than those you came across later, and the final trace they leave will be stronger. However, it isn't *always* the first that makes the biggest impact. The context is important, too. Impact is generally higher when your emotions are heightened, so the song that was playing when you first fell in love, or when you celebrated your exam results, is likely to stick with you for longer than all the others.

You might think that memories from your early childhood would have the biggest impact of all, but this is not the case. For many events, it is the ones you experienced in your late teens and early twenties as you emerged into adulthood that have the biggest impact. When a group of Americans were asked to name the most historic event in their lifetime, adults born around 1910 tended to say the Depression, those born in the 1920s said the Second World War, those born in the 1940s said the assassination of John F. Kennedy, and those in the 1950s the Vietnam War.

Faulty replication

A memory may be stored accurately and be free from any obvious interference, yet it is still vulnerable to being distorted somewhere along the way.

When you are recalling any incident from your past, you might like to consider what it is that you are actually remembering. The exact chemistry of what a memory comprises isn't understood, but one theory is that what you are remembering is not the original fact or incident. What you are remembering is *the last time you remembered* that incident.

If you imagine your initial memory of something as a photocopy, then when you subsequently recall that memory it is the copy that you are recalling. Each time you recall the memory thereafter, you are retrieving a copy of a copy of a copy. All it takes is for a copy to get distorted in some way and all subsequent recollections will themselves be distorted. If you have recalled an incident a hundred times, you will become convinced that it is a genuine memory, but if the corruption to the memory happened right at the beginning, all you have been doing is accurately recalling a false memory a hundred times.

This might explain the experience of a friend who recalled visiting the Science Museum with his father to see an 'economic computer' driven by water. He later discovered that the museum couldn't possibly have had this device at the time he made the visit, so somewhere in his past his memory of the incident got corrupted. Maybe the so-called memory was no more than a wish that had never been fulfilled.

One thing that we all remember is where we were when the news of historic world events first broke. Except that, astonishingly, researchers have found that even these memories become distorted. So-called 'flash-bulb' memory – where you were and what you were doing when a significant event happened in your past – is frequently inaccurate. Your memory of the event itself (John F. Kennedy's assassination, Princess Diana's funeral, 9/11) is probably vivid, but where you were and what you were doing can often be much shakier. How do we know this? Because people record in their diaries where they were and what they were doing, and this can be checked against what they *say* they were doing that day. Often the two don't match, yet people trust their memory so much that when confronted with the written evidence, it is apparently common for people to say that it is the written evidence that is wrong rather than the image that they recall.

All in all, it is clear that there is plenty of scope for our memories to play tricks with us.

Deliberate memory distortion

These examples of memory interference beg the question of how much we can rely on any memory that we have, unless there is independent evidence such as a photograph to confirm it. Fortunately, more often than not the more important details of those things we concentrate on are accurately recalled.

Sometimes, however, we deliberately change a memory to suit our own purposes; for example, to make an anecdote more memorable or an excuse more convincing. When a great raconteur tells the story of how 'that lion jumped out and it was as far from me as you are right now' I seriously doubt that the reality was anything close to this, but equally I am prepared to believe that the teller is now convinced that the story is quite true. On a more mundane level, when somebody says 'I kept trying to call you over the weekend but your number was busy', I'm prepared to believe it happened once or twice over a five-minute period, but not over the whole weekend.

I have noticed myself manipulating my past in this way on a couple of occasions. I once played in a cricket match at which one of the two umpires was a minor member of the royal family. That day I was given out leg before wicket, not by the earl's son but by the other umpire, one of my team-mates, making it an anecdote not quite worthy of the name-drop. Of course when it came to telling people about my experience, it made for a much better story to report that I'd been given out by a future earl. I recall telling people my slightly modified version of the truth, which I like to think of as a sort of artistic licence. The bizarre thing is that despite the fact that I know he didn't raise the finger on the day, when I now picture that incident I can actually visualise the earl's son standing at the far end giving me out. I've clearly managed to etch this false story into my memory. Who knows on how many other occasions I have made such adjustments less consciously?

Tip-of-the-tongue syndrome

Perhaps the most frustrating aspect of a declining memory is the familiar situation of trying to recall a piece of information, usually a word, and being unable to do so – while at the same time *knowing* that you know it, and feeling that you are tantalisingly 'close' to it. Instead of calling this 'forgetting', you might call it 'not being quite able to remember'. There's a subtle difference!

This state of having something 'on the tip of your tongue' has been researched in some detail, so quite a lot is now known about it as a condition, with a few theories as to why it happens. Tip of the tongue affects most people over the age of 30, and tends to become more noticeable as we age. The normal tip-of-the-tongue experience tends to be that we can feel what kind of word it is we are on the verge of retrieving. 'It's a long word', or 'it's sort of Italian-sounding', or even 'it begins with T'.

One theory as to why this happens is that when we are trying to remember a word, we first remember the image associated with it, and then use that image to link to the sound of the word that goes with it. The problem arises when the link between image and sound are not strong enough, and typically this will happen when there are various similar sounds competing for your attention. If the link to the correct word is not strong enough, then when fishing around for the right word you might stumble across one that is similar, and having made that incorrect link, it then becomes increasingly difficult to think of the correct one. It's almost as if the wrong word is deliberately stealing the place of the right one.

A Hard Time with 'Home Truths'

I encountered a recurring tip-of-the-tongue experience for over a year when trying to think of the title of an old Saturday morning BBC radio programme presented by the late John Peel. I can now say with confidence that the programme was called *Home Truths* but only because my failure to remember it in the past became such a big issue! When the block first arose I would struggle for up to a minute trying to recall the name. The problem was that for years the Saturday morning programme that I listened to over breakfast had been called *Loose Ends*. To me, *Loose Ends* and *Home Truths* sound very similar. They are both short, two-word, everyday terms. When trying to think of the name *Home Truths* I would invariably find myself blocked by *Loose Ends*. I would then try a different route, getting as far as H---- T----, only to then come up with the title *Hard Times* !

Some psychologists believe that once a wrong word has surfaced, it actually serves as a block, dominating your memory sufficiently to actually suppress the correct answer. The only way to overcome this block is to divert your mind onto something else for a few moments. With the dominant wrong answer subsiding away from the working memory, the mind pursues different associations that link through to the right answer. Often, as if by magic, the right answer will suddenly pop up (no doubt you have had this experience many times).

Some words are more likely to end up on the tip of our tongue than others. Top of the list are the names of people (extremely often), followed by titles of books, films and other 'proper names' or technical terms (less often). It is much less common for the tip-of-tongue word to belong to an object such as, say, a sofa.

The reason for this is simple. When describing the furniture in my lounge, if I happen to have a momentary block on the word 'sofa' there are other words that will do instead. 'Couch' and 'settee' are both adequate substitutes. I won't report a tip-of-the-tongue experience in this case because my hesitation was so brief I barely noticed it.

This is not the case for most names. If I know somebody called Joan, that is likely to be the only name by which I know her. There is no substitute. Jane, Jenny or 'That blonde woman with the big teeth' are all quite unacceptable ways of addressing her. So of course if I do stumble, I'm really going to notice the tip-of-tongue experience, and be frustrated by it.

It's also believed that we store words by their individual sounds, not the whole sound. This means that you don't store the word Timbuktu as a single chunk, but rather as several bites of sound, T –im –buk –tu, in a chain. T links to –im, which links to –buk, which links to –tu. Once you've happened upon the 'T' sound at the beginning, there's a higher chance that the rest of the word will be triggered in stages, which is why running through the alphabet can be a helpful aid when confronted by a tip-of-the-tongue moment.

If You Think Your Story is Embarrassing ... Part 3, Royal Blush

So-called senior moments happen to the great and famous, too. One of my favourite stories concerns the great musical conductor Sir Thomas Beecham, who was at a function at a hotel in Manchester in the 1930s. He found himself next to a woman whom he thought he recognised. Struggling to think of something to talk about, he remembered that the woman had a brother.. 'Tell me, how is your brother? Is he still doing the same job?'

'He's very well, thank you,' she replied, 'and yes, he is still the king.'

Part Two:

The Fundamentals to Improving Your Memory

5
The Motivation to Improve Your Memory

Topics covered

- Rate your memory (is it as bad as you think it is?)
- What do you need to remember?
- Passive and active memory

Most of us care enough about our ability to remember to want to preserve it. Many people go further and express a wish to *improve* it, though a common attitude seems to be summed up by Greg, who told me: 'What I'd like is some quick fixes to improve my everyday memory, but which *don't require any effort.*'

This statement seems to be the crux of the matter, and as I mentioned in Chapter 1, this might explain why many people become disillusioned with programmes that promise to turn you into a super-memoriser. Many of these programmes require a substantial investment of time both in learning the techniques and then in practising them. They may also need a commitment to certain changes in behaviour or even in lifestyle. These are not easy changes to make for any but the most dedicated, which probably explains why memory books often lie gathering dust on the shelf, while the techniques that they espouse for boosting memory are quietly forgotten.

So, before embarking on the road to memory improvement, I recommend three steps of preparation.

Rating your memory (is it as bad as you think it is?)

One of the interesting things that has emerged when psychologists research memory is how poor many people are at assessing their own abilities. When groups are asked to first of all rate their own memory, and then to take a series of tests on verbal and visual memory tasks, there is often little correlation between the two results.

It would seem that some people who rate their memory as extremely good simply *forget* just *how often they forget*. Meanwhile, those who spot every time their memory fails them – and report that incident to their friends, or even their doctor – are often indirectly showing just how sharp their memory is, to be able to recall these incidents in such detail. 'Doctor, last Tuesday I quite forgot that Becky goes to ballet class, and yesterday I realised I'd forgotten my mobile phone so I had to make all my client phone calls from a payphone.'

It's also important to take account of the context in which people are rating their memories. If you plot the graph of how highly people rate their memories, it can typically show a downward trend as they move towards their 50s, but then actually pick up again towards their 70s.

What is the explanation for this improvement? Almost certainly, it is nothing to do with the person's actual memory competence. The 70-year-olds are likely to perform less well in memory tests than the 50-year-olds. Instead, it is all down to the stage people are at in their careers.

At the age of 50, many people are in responsible jobs, which can require them to keep a handle on a huge number of different tasks, as well as details about those people who report to them. With all of these things that put demands on memory, including the stress of the job itself, there is plenty of opportunity every day for a memory lapse. On top of that, memory lapses in the workplace can be costly. A client might be offended when you forget to turn up to a meeting, there could be an expensive accident caused by forgetting to close a valve … and so on. No wonder the 50-year-old, surrounded by quick-minded juniors in their twenties, is extremely conscious of any defects in her memory.

Compare that with the 70-year-old, sat at home watching daytime TV, popping down to the Post Office as he does every Tuesday, and going for lunch in the regular pub with other retired friends. This routine life throws up far fewer occasions where memory is such an issue. That's not to say that those incidents don't happen, but they are less likely to happen than they are to the busy executive at a desk. It is no surprise, therefore, that a 70-year-old might declare himself 'content' with his memory, while a 50-year-old is 'worried'.

Rating yourself against other people can sometimes

create an anxiety that you otherwise didn't have. Think of that friend with the ability to recall in intricate detail the holiday you took ten years ago, including the itinerary, the meals you ate, the people you met, and the pictures that were hanging in the restaurant. Or the aunt who never forgets a birthday, and always picks the perfect present to suit your particular interest of the moment. Or the medic who somehow manages to absorb a shelf-full of Latin names for the most obscure illnesses and body parts, despite seemingly spending most of his student days in the bar.

Comparing yourself against people like this can be a humbling experience, sometimes prompting a feeling of inadequacy. How come they can remember all these things, and I can't? Am I losing it?

There's probably a name for this syndrome, or if there isn't, you can call it 'selective envy disorder' (or SED), a tendency to notice and be envious of only those people who appear better in some way, while ignoring the many counter-examples. It applies in many walks of life, though some cause more anxiety than others.

Yes, we all know people who can perform astounding memory feats. We all know, or at least know of, people who can run a four-minute mile, too. In any group, there will always be people with exceptional abilities. But for every super-fit person or super-memory person you know, you can probably think of five or ten who are anything but. Memory, intelligence, physical fitness, the ability to cook – none of these are black-and-white things you are 'good' or 'bad' at, but instead they lie on a spectrum. Rather than setting out to be the best, it's more helpful to think about how you can move yourself along the spectrum.

I have included a questionnaire in Appendix 1 that will enable you to make a rough assessment of your memory. You may surprise yourself and discover that your memory is exceptional compared to the norm, but it is more likely that you are as prone to some memory lapses as everyone else. In the unlikely event that your self-assessment suggests that your memory is alarmingly poor, there are practical things you can do about it.

If It's Not Worrying You, It's Not a Problem

How 'good' your memory is can all be down to attitude. I have a friend, Clive, who is perfectly happy with his memory. While researching this book, I asked him if his elderly parents would be prepared to help me in researching memory and aging. He said he was sure they would be delighted, and that he would ask them that evening.

The next day when I prompted him, he said he'd forgotten to ask them, but was seeing them again that day and so would definitely ask them this time. Once again, nothing was forthcoming, and we didn't discuss it again.

So Clive had twice forgotten to perform a task he said he would do. But is this a problem? I would say that it is only a problem if he thinks it is a problem. Perhaps the task was very low on his list of priorities. Or maybe he failed to firmly register what he'd agreed to do. You only worry about such things if you (a) remember that you forgot, and (b) you care enough about what happened that the forgetting actually matters to you.

What do you need to remember?

As a result of the previous section, you might now be feeling more relaxed about the state of your memory. On the other hand, it might have reinforced your desire to do something about it. But memory improvement is a huge field, and before embarking on it, you should spend a moment or two thinking about where you would like to focus your efforts.

I've sung the praises of the brain and its astonishing powers to absorb and regurgitate relevant information, but let's not get carried away with the need to commit everything to our mental store. Sometimes too much emphasis is put on the brain to remember things for the sake of doing so.

I sent out a questionnaire to a cross-section of people asking them, among other things, what techniques they used to remember important facts. One respondent, Andrew, had a pithy response: 'I write them down.'

Well, why not? Mankind has invented all sorts of aids to make life more comfortable, and a pen and paper are among the most useful. If you need to know when Isaac Newton was born, then the most important thing is not to have memorised the fact, but to know where the best place is to look it up. This isn't going to be much help if you are taking part in a quiz, but fortunately life isn't all about competing in *The Weakest Link*.

So before going any further, it's worth pausing to think about what information you *need* to commit to memory. Clearly there are some pieces of information without which it becomes almost impossible to function or to interact socially unless you carry them around in your head. These include, for example, your name and address, where the shops are, how to open a tin of baked beans ... and other such crucial nuggets. Fortunately few of us have too many problems with these bare essentials.

Everything else that you 'need to know' can now be put in a hierarchy of importance. I find it helpful to put them into four categories, and to represent them as a target (see Diagram 2). The things you most need to remember are at the centre of the target, and those with lower importance are progressively further out. The four headings I like to use are Critical, Reassuring, Aspirational and Peripheral. (It occurs to me that these words form a rather crude but memorable acronym, which I won't bother to spell out!)

Diagram 2: Hierarchy of information

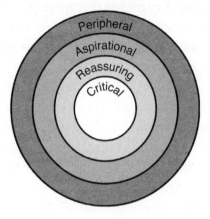

Critical

This is the information that you need to be able to retrieve almost instantly in order to live and work in the way you want to. Everyone has some specific pieces of knowledge that are vital for them to operate success-fully. A GP will struggle if she has to look up every disease symptom and drug. A simultaneous translator depends on having a wide knowledge of two vocabu-laries at his fingertips. Anyone working in a team needs to have names and other key information about colleagues to hand. Because they are so important to you, you probably have little trouble remembering any of these things. If you do have difficulty then this is, needless to say, the main area for you to concentrate on, where investment in time and energy will have the biggest reward.

Reassuring

Under this broad category come things where forgetting can be awkward or embarrassing, but you are still able to conduct your everyday affairs with reasonable competence. Where did I leave the keys? What is my PIN number? What's the name of the British Prime Minister? What is the collective noun for cows? Although you don't have to have this information at your fingertips, doing so enables you to carry out routine functions quickly and efficiently, and also helps you to engage rather more fully in conversation without interspersing every sentence with 'What's his name?' and 'Er ... you know'. Can you think of situations where failing to remember cause you stress or embarrassment? Are you prepared to put in some time to improve things?

Aspirational

This category represents part of life's great wish list. *You wish* you could remember even half the recipes for meals you have eaten. *You wish* you could remember the storylines in all those Shakespeare plays you have seen. *You wish* you knew the capital cities and customs of all the major countries in the world. If you had this information at your fingertips, it would make you more versatile, and would enrich the conversations that you have with new people that you meet. It might even help to make a good impression if you were seeking to make friends and influence people.

But at the moment your memory of all these things is

patchy at best, and if you want this situation to change then you have to face up to the fact that you are going to have to do something about it. After all, if this information hasn't stuck so far, it is unreasonable to expect that it will suddenly stick now. So you are confronted with the question: Just how much do you really want to know these things? Is the knowledge gained worth the trade-off with time exerted? Maybe your response is: 'Hmm, I'll think about it, but unless there are some instant remedies, I've got some other more important things to get on with ...'

Peripheral

This is probably the biggest category of all. There is a ton of information out there to absorb that isn't of any interest to you and that you can see little or no advantage in knowing. Maybe it's the different models of Ford car for example, or the bulbs that should be planted in October, or the order of nerves that pass through the superior orbital tissue in the skull. (It's a pity about the last one, because the sentence 'Lazy French Tarts Lie Naked in Anticipation' is very handy in helping to recall this information, or so I'm told.) And if you are not interested and the information has no relevance to you, you should lose no sleep over the fact that you can't remember it. What can be annoying, of course, is that your brain may contain lots of information in which you have no particular interest and which is of no obvious use. High on the list of redundant information rattling around up there will be advertising jingles you absorbed as a child – a testament to the skills of the advertising industry in getting this information into you in the first place.

Prioritising what you need to remember is an important first step in establishing just how motivated you are to improve your memory. Clearly it is among the items in categories 1 and 2, *Critical* and *Reassuring*, that your priorities should lie, and where there is an obvious reason to put in some effort. For the other two categories, it's only going to be worth remembering the information if to do so is an enjoyable and straightforward task.

In conducting my informal survey of people's concerns about memory, some aspects cropped up as areas of anxiety far more often than others. Table 2 (overleaf) shows the top ten concerns that were expressed to me, which range from general areas of worry to others that are much more specific.

Names came top by a long way. In fact, well over half the people I have asked about memory explicitly mentioned their inability to remember names as their main concern. A few mentioned that while they remember names, they don't remember faces. Numbers featured quite low in the list, though that is partly because people often said, 'I'm so hopeless with numbers, I don't even bother'. (Maybe there is hope – see Chapter 11.)

Table 2 gives a good indication of where most people's priorities lie, and all of these issues are examined in later chapters.

Table 2: Which area of your memory is of most concern to you? (The top ten responses)

Remembering the names of people
Short-term forgetfulness of tasks, etc.
Appointments later in the day
'Is my memory loss normal?'
Birthdays/other important dates
Jokes
Numbers
Past events
Learning a new subject
Stories and histories

Passive and active memory

The fact that effort is required to remember things comes as a disappointment to some people. This is because when we are young (up to the age of about 30), memory appears to work without us even thinking about it. We get used to the idea that remembering lyrics, destinations, names, film plots and even foreign vocabulary is almost effort*less*. I refer to this form of memory as *passive* because it appears to happen without doing anything. Memory seems to just stick without any conscious effort.

By our mid-30s, as tip-of-tongue and other memory lapses become commonplace, we are understandably frustrated that things aren't like they used to be. Passive memory no longer seems to be sufficient. It's no different from discovering that the body will no longer stand up to physical challenges or a heavy night out on the town, but somehow the popular view is that brains aren't supposed to go the same way (at least, not until we're old and doddery).

If you want to maintain your everyday ability to remember things, memorising and recalling has to become a more conscious or *active* process, particularly above the age of about 35. It is this transition from passive to active that is at the centre of most important aide-memoirs.

This shift may be harder for those people born since the 1970s. Some younger adults I have spoken to can recall no occasions where they were required to sit down and memorise facts. If you have little experience of memorising it does mean that when confronted with the need to memorise later in life, you might have fewer familiar strategies available to tackle the problem.

When Greg said to me 'I want to improve my memory without much effort', what he was really saying was 'I want to improve my passive memory'. I can't promise that this can be achieved without some effort (that is to say, to improve your passive memory you do have to take some actions first) but the strategies in the next few chapters should help. With practice, you begin to use memory aids without even realising that you are doing so.

How Stephanie Addressed Her Memory Worries

If you are looking for a low-effort way to deal with your memory worries, you could follow the example of Stephanie, who told me with delight how she had dealt with her memory anxieties when in her mid-30s. At the time, Stephanie had a young family and was becoming increasingly concerned about her memory lapses. She was forgetting dates and people's names, and felt as though she was no longer able to concentrate on story lines in books and TV programmes.

So she decided to do something about it. She began to make a point of registering people's names when she met them and then testing herself on the names later in the day. Each morning she thought through what she had to do during the day, then checked her diary and marked herself on how well she had remembered. It became almost an obsession.

After about a week, she had convinced herself that there was actually nothing wrong with her memory. When she had put her mind to it, she had realised she was quite capable of remembering all the things that she wanted to. As a result, she told me, her anxiety subsided. She stopped using the memory techniques she adopted (too much effort, she felt), knowing that *if she wanted to* she would be able to pick them up again.

Is her memory any better now that she has lapsed to her more casual, passive approach? Possibly not. But she is less worried about it, which, to her, is just as important.

6
How to Keep Your Brain Healthy

Topics covered

- Four ways to kill your memory
- Physical health
- Mental exercise
- Stress and anxiety
- Memory food
- Drugs
- Herbal remedies

Four ways to kill your memory

One thing that is fundamental to a good memory is the health of the brain in which it sits. You can't expect to run a mile if your body is out of shape, and the same applies to mental functions and your brain.

Let's play opposites for a moment, and imagine that for some reason you wanted to kill off your ability to remember anything, either in the short term or the long term. What would be the most efficient way to dumb your memory down? I can think of four key steps to killing your memory.

One is a physical pummelling. Trauma to the head can permanently damage brain cells. That's why in the long term boxers are more prone to Parkinson's and other brain diseases, and it seems that footballers who regularly head the ball are also vulnerable to this problem.

Another step to killing off the brain is intoxication. Alcohol is the most readily available substance for this, and not only does it slow down the brain's functions when it is in the blood, in excess it also has a known detrimental effect on the brain's health in the long term, because it kills brain cells. The impact of other 'recreational' drugs on memory in the long term is less cut and dried, but watching old rock stars being interviewed and giving their slurred, slow answers to questions, it's clear that whatever other brain functions might be aided by the taking of drugs, mental agility is not among them.

The third way to help the decline of the brain is to ignore it. There is increasing scientific evidence that sitting watching TV or otherwise vegetating causes the brain to decline, simply because if it is not being stimulated then its cells deteriorate. It appears that the phrase 'use it or lose it' really does apply to the brain.

Finally, the food that you eat can be important to the health of the brain. A diet of burgers and highly salted chips is probably the best combination for brain decay, both because it avoids feeding the brain the nutrients that help it to function, and, more importantly, because this sort of diet increases the risk of heart disease and strokes, with the latter particularly effective at knocking out brain function and memory.

Well, so much for this game of negatives. What are the positive things you can do to nurture a healthy brain?

Physical fitness

One of the best ways of recovering from mental exhaustion can be physical exercise. A demanding hike up a mountain may be tiring, but it does seem to freshen up the brain, partly by allowing it to mull over some of the issues that have been taxing it recently.

As strategies for improving your ability to remember go, taking a jog around the park may seem one of the least obvious, yet it can have both short-term and long-term benefits. Getting out of the office or the house and going for a jog or stroll is one way of stepping back and allowing your mind to wander, which is one of the most effective ways of overcoming a tip-of-the-tongue problem. On top of that, you are exposing yourself to more random stimulants that might remind you of things you had forgotten about. A familiar face, an item in a shop window or the colour of a door may be just the cue to trigger an associated memory that leads to the thing you were trying to remember (or maybe even the thing you *weren't* trying to remember, but are glad you did!) It gives a whole meaning to the expression 'jog your memory'.

Physical fitness also helps to reduce weight and blood pressure, and in turn this will reduce the risks of damage to the brain later in life. The third benefit of taking exercise is that it can help you to sleep. Tiredness can slow down all cognitive functions including the ability to learn and to retrieve memories. Physical exhaustion followed by deep sleep is great therapy for the brain.

Mental exercise

Crossword fans swear by the benefits to be had from a daily dose of word play. They believe that it helps to keep their brains active and alert. And there is more than anecdotal evidence to support this view.

One piece of evidence is the so-called 'Nun Study'. In 1986, David Snowdon and colleagues from the University of Minnesota began an investigation into the factors that might lead to Alzheimer's disease. Their study concentrated on a community of nuns, who had all kept diaries of their activities since their early twenties. This study, which continues to this day, has revealed a considerable amount of information about how brains age, including the role of mental stimulation.

The evidence looks convincing. Those nuns who were the best educated, as evidenced by the quality and richness of their writing when they were young, showed considerably fewer signs of Alzheimer's than their less well-educated peers. The simple conclusion, therefore, is that education (and the brain-stretching that it involves) reduces or delays the risk of Alzheimer's disease.

However, the scientists are quick to point out that there are other ways to interpret these results. For example, it could be that those who are born with well-connected, agile brains are less vulnerable to Alzheimer's later in life, and by having good brains it is no surprise that these people will tend to be the ones most likely to go on to higher education. In other words, while it might be true that education delays the onset of Alzheimer's, it might instead just be that low risk Alzheimer's brains belong to those who go into higher education.

Nonetheless, the weight of opinion is that education does improve long-term brain health. The reason for this might be explained by neurological studies into the structure of brains that have been stimulated versus those that haven't. Tests on rats have shown that rats that are deprived of stimulation end up with smaller brains than those that are given plenty of stimulation in the form of wheels, toys and a varied diet. The stimulation seems to result in more neurons and synapses being formed in the rats' brains to cope with the extra demands.

Similar results seem to apply to humans. New forms of scan, especially Positron emission tomography (the PET scan) indicate that brains that have been stimulated by regular activities such as doing jigsaws, solving crosswords and indulging in handicrafts show greater activity than their counterparts when faced with other mental challenges. It seems that regular mental exercise builds up the brain in the same way that physical exercise builds muscles and strengthens the heart.

Of course the techniques for aiding memory described in this book are also forms of mental stimulation. Such devices as the room method (see page 176) are generally viewed as ways to aid the memory, but maybe it's more helpful to regard them as a type of mental game. You can start to use memory techniques to learn shopping lists not because you need to, but because you find it fun and it exercises the brain.

If you find that these memory techniques work, they have another benefit, namely that they leave you feeling good about your ability to remember. After all, who wouldn't be pleased with themselves for accurately remembering a list of twenty items forwards and backwards, regardless of whether it has much practical value?

Stress and anxiety

There are people in every age group who admit to having some concern about the failings in their memory. And of course, the more worried you are about your memory, the greater your motivation is for doing something about it.

As I mentioned earlier, this level of anxiety seems to reach a peak around the age of 50, a combination of the natural decline in certain mental abilities with age and the extra demands on memory that some jobs bring with increasing responsibility.

The problem with anxiety about memory is that it is a self-fulfilling mental state. One of the things that most disrupts the ability to recall information is being anxious. Hormones released when you are under stress have been found to temporarily suppress the ability to retrieve information from your long- and short-term memory.

You have almost certainly experienced this, for example in school exams when your head felt like it was spinning and you couldn't think of that French word or that chemical reaction. (Yet as soon as you stepped out of the exam room, the answer came to you.) Or think of the time when you gave a speech, and suddenly all those well-chosen words disappeared, leaving your mind blank.

Worrying about memory therefore leads to poor performance in memory tests, which is in danger of creating even more anxiety. It's a vicious circle.

If your current lifestyle is filled with unwanted stress and anxiety, making you short-tempered and sleepless, your ability to remember is bound to suffer. Recognising what it is that is causing you stress is the first step to addressing the problem.

Memory food

A good diet can help memory in a number of ways:

- in helping concentration in the short term, which means memories are more likely to be formed accurately in the first place;

81

- in boosting the appropriate chemicals in the brain to keep it healthy and alert when it comes to storing and retrieving information; and, quite possibly,
- to avert some of the factors that might lead to the early onset of Alzheimer's disease.

However, many of the claims about food and the brain need to be treated with caution. Since I began researching this book, there have been several stories in the news about how food can improve memory. The first story was that scientists had discovered that eating breakfast was good for the memory (see 'The Breakfast Factor' box). This was followed by stories about red meat and the herb sage, which it emerged has been 'known' for centuries to be an aid to memory.

Who knows how many other such stories I missed, or indeed how many more foods will have been claimed by scientists to aid memory by the time this book is in your hands? Before making instant changes to your diet, it is perhaps worth asking where these stories come from, and what they actually mean.

Then there is the question of *what aspect* of memory is being boosted by a particular food. We already know that memory is a very broad field. There's short- and long-term memory, the ability to remember the important facts rather than the peripherals, and so on. In the case of sage, what the scientists found was that, when tested for word recall after consuming sage oil capsules, people in their twenties performed consistently better than their peers who were given placebos. So what does this tell us about sage and memory? Perhaps that it helps short-term memory for young adults; maybe by helping them to concentrate, or by stimulating the brain to make it more receptive. But does consuming sage capsules make it more likely that you will be able to remember the name of a familiar person when you bump into them in the street? This is an altogether different issue, to which we don't know the answer, though I think it highly unlikely that sage capsules on their own will be the answer to anyone's memory problems.

The Breakfast Factor

The much-publicised claim that breakfast is good for the memory came from genuine research by scientists, but the research was funded by a body called Cereal Partners UK. Now, if you were a group called Cereal Partners funding research into breakfast, what sort of results would you want to see come out of the study? That corn flakes dull the mind and lead to unruly behaviour? I think not. So while I don't doubt the authenticity of the research, perhaps the news story doesn't present us with the full picture. (For example, *how much* difference does breakfast make? Does eating a mid-morning snack of crisps and cola have just as good an impact? How does bacon and eggs fare compared to cereal?) It is wise to question any findings until you discover exactly who it is that was behind the research. Independent studies by groups with no particular axe to grind are on the whole more credible.

Beneath all the hype, there is some more solid advice about food that is healthy for the brain and that could aid memory:

- **Fish.** If you wanted to reduce a good brain diet to one word, it would be the word 'fish'. And if you wanted a good brain diet in two words, it is 'oily fish'. Oily fish is the top scorer in foods that contain 'Omega-3' unsaturates (see below). Tuna, salmon, herring and trout get special mentions. Fish also contains a fatty acid called DHA which increases the levels of acetyl-choline, a vital carrier involved in the brain's memory function. Strong claims are made of fish oil, including one that it can help to alleviate some of the symptoms of Alzheimer's patients, though this claim should still be regarded as speculation. Catholics have traditionally eaten fish on Fridays. The Food Standards Agency goes one further, and recommends fish twice a week in a good diet. And if you can face it on Fridays, Mondays and Wednesdays, that is probably even better!
- **Unsaturated fats.** Unsaturated fats are an important part of the brain's make-up, and they are derived directly from our diet. In general, unsaturated fats are deemed to be good for the diet, but there is a sub-group of these fats known as 'Omega-3' unsaturated fats that have gained a reputation as being particu-larly 'good' fats because (it is claimed) they improve the chemical balance in the brain, and reduce the risks of brain inflammation caused by excessive

amounts of one of the other unsaturated fats, 'Omega-6'. Foods high in Omega-3 fats include flax-seed oil and walnuts.

- **Foods containing antioxidants.** The world is full of nasty things called free radicals that, if we absorb too many of them, can cause fundamental damage to our bodies, including our brains and our DNA. Fortunately there is a knight in shining armour that can see off the excess of free radicals. That knight is called an antioxidant. The biochemistry gets quite complicated, but suffice to say, foods with antioxidants are good things. High on the list come foods packed with Vitamin C – such as orange juice and fresh fruit and vegetables – and Vitamin E – such as walnuts, almonds, wheat germ and sunflower oil. Prunes also come highly recommended, as does tea, especially green tea.

- **Carbohydrate/sugar boosts.** Carbohydrates help to improve your alertness and therefore your ability to form new memories and to retrieve old ones. Simple carbohydrates such as glucose are easy for the body to break down, and they can therefore provide a quick boost, though this will also wear off quite quickly. Complex carbohydrates, as found in bread and cereals, are harder for the body to break down, and they therefore have a more modest but longer-lasting effect. So, if you are preparing for a short memory test in a few minutes time you might try eating a bar of chocolate, but if you have a three-hour exam you are better off eating a bowl of muesli.

So is all this pointing to an ideal diet for the memory? You could do worse than start the day with a breakfast comprising orange juice, prunes, kippers with tomatoes and bread, and a cup of green tea (without milk).

Of course, the fact is that we are physiologically different from each other, and what benefits one person will not necessarily benefit the next. Although *on average for a large group of people* fish, unsaturated fats, antioxidants and carbohydrates will lead to an overall boost to average memory performance in the short and long term, whether they will work for an individual depends very much on that person's make-up. If you can't bear fish, or it brings you out in an allergic rash, there's no benefit in force-feeding yourself on it. One of the brightest people I know never eats any breakfast, and still manages to hold up a very responsible, brain-taxing job which suggests that it is, at very least, *possible* for some people to function perfectly well without any breakfast.

Does Eating Food Cooked in Aluminium Saucepans Damage Your Memory?

A couple of studies in the last 40 years claimed to have found a slight link between the number of cases of Alzheimer's and the amount of aluminium in the environment. Scare stories emerged that suggested cooking with aluminium saucepans was seriously increasing the risks. To this day, there are people who refuse to have any aluminium implements in the kitchen.

However, scientists have had time to gather more evidence since those earlier investigations, and the overwhelming view among scientists today is that aluminium poses no risk. If you throw out your aluminium pans all you are doing is wasting a very helpful implement.

Drugs

The newest and most rapidly developing area of brain health is the use of drugs to boost memory. Drugs to help patients with Alzheimer's disease have been around for many years but since the 1990s, interest in them has grown enormously as new avenues for the treatment of memory disorders have opened up.
Broadly, memory drugs help in one of two ways:

- boosting the natural substances in the brain that are crucial to the memory process; or
- inhibiting the processes that are causing the brain to degenerate.

If you hear a drug being described as 'memory-boosting', be careful to read the small print. At best, the claim is likely to mean that the drug improves your ability to record memories in the first place. That's very different from boosting your ability to *retrieve* memories. So, a drug *might* enable you to commit to memory more items than you would have stored otherwise, but it won't suddenly bring back memories of what you learned in your biology class, or where you left the keys.

One of the substances that is believed to be essential in the formation of memories is acetylcholine (as is found in fish oil), and some treatments involve boosting either this substance directly or in managing the enzymes that help to create or destroy it. One such drug is Donepezil (often branded as Aricept), which is prescribed to people diagnosed as being in the early stages of Alzheimer's disease. It is not a cure, but is found to slow down the progress of the disease in many patients.

There has been much speculation about whether hormone replacement therapy (HRT) can help memory. There is evidence that post-menopausal women on HRT perform better in memory tests than those not taking the drug, but this may have more to do with the people taking the drug than the drug itself. For those aged over 65, the growing evidence is that HRT does not aid memory, and may even accelerate its decline.

Other memory drugs are built around:

- antioxidants, aimed at preventing the damage to brain cells caused by free radicals,
- anti-amyloids, which help to remove the plaques and tangles associated with Alzheimer's; or

- anti-inflammatories, which prevent the damage caused by brain inflammation.

The claims being made for the power of these drugs are increasingly dramatic, particularly in the USA where advertisements for brain-boosting remedies (both prescribed and herbal) are ever-present, particularly in TV programmes and magazines aimed at the older, more affluent age groups.

While there are certainly drugs that are known to help *some* people with *some* memory conditions, their impact is generally quite small and short-term, which means that users need to take the pills regularly to experience a sustained improvement to their memory. Patients expecting to see a restoration of their old powers of memory will usually be disappointed, leading to comments like one from Natalie, who has been taking one such drug for several months: 'As far as I can tell, the only reason I take these pills is so that I can remember to take these pills!' Many of these drugs can also have unpleasant side-effects (these will be different depending on the particular drug).

Still, new discoveries are being made all the time, and it's worth checking up on a reliable source on the Web if you want to know about whether any drugs have been found that have genuine memory-enhancing properties.

Herbal remedies

Many people choose to avoid prescribed drugs and use herbal remedies instead. The most famous, and by far the most popular, is ginkgo biloba. Ginkgo is extracted from the leaves of the Chinese ginkgo tree, and has entered folklore as being a memory-enhancer. It has become a massively popular treatment for memory impairment, particularly in Germany and the USA.

Often the drugs beloved of folklore have little scientific evidence to support them, but in the case of ginkgo it seems that there is a definite, if small, benefit to taking it. Groups of adults were found to score 10–20 per cent better in certain memory tests after consuming ginkgo. Before getting too excited about this, it's worth knowing that the glucose boost from a bar of chocolate can have a similar impact. Exactly how ginkgo helps memory is unclear. It could simply be that it reduces anxiety, and therefore aids concentration and retention. Perhaps it has a short-term effect on the receptiveness of the brain.

One finding is consistent with the majority of memory drugs and herbal remedies. In the short term, perhaps for a few weeks, there can be a measurable improvement in memory simply due to the comfort of knowing that one is taking something that is claimed to have memory-enhancing benefits. This is what is commonly referred to as the *placebo effect*. For a period of time, placebo pills perform just as well as the leading drug Donepezil, though after a while the performance of those patients who are unknowingly on the placebo treatment begins to fall away faster than that of the Donepezil patients.

But the message from this is clear. So long as you believe that a drug treatment is improving your memory, for a while it genuinely will do so, regardless of whether or not there is any scientific basis for it.

7
Organising for a Better Memory

Topics covered

- How organising helps
- Categorising before you store
- Brain-mapping
- Remembering where you left something
- Organising for disorganised people

By 'having a better memory' most people mean 'being able to retrieve information better'. Of course you don't have to be a genius to realise that you can only retrieve information if it's actually there in the first place.

One crucial step to a better memory is better organisation.

This chapter looks at some of the simple, if unglamorous, steps you can take to help you to organise for a better memory.

A Good Memory?

Sometimes what appears to be a remarkable memory is not all that it seems. Take Henry Whitehouse, for example. For years, Henry was the man in charge of recruitment at one of Britain's largest professional firms. This firm recruited over 100 graduates every

---

year, and each recruit would have a joining interview with Henry. By the time he retired he had met literally thousands of fresh-faced newcomers.

What so impressed those recruits was that those who bumped into him again, sometimes years later, would find that he not only remembered who they were, but also personal details such as where they had joined from.

What few people knew about Henry was that he kept an intricate card system. Every time he met a new graduate he would create a card, put their photo on it, and add a few salient details about their background and anything of note that had come up in their conversation. By the time he retired, his card system filled a whole cabinet of drawers. Every so often he'd spend an evening just flicking through his old records. While you or I were at home watching TV or playing with the children, he'd be looking at the list of invitees to the next day's reunion party, compiling their crib cards, and reminding himself of the subjects he should be raising – or avoiding – when he got into conversation with them.

There are many words that you could use to describe Henry's abilities. Meticulous and highly organised come to mind, for example. By the normal, narrow definition of memory, however, we wouldn't describe him as having astounding powers of recall. Yet the outward effect is the same. Like the Wizard of Oz, when you discover the secrets of the all-powerful ones, their magical powers seem more attainable to all of us.

How organising helps

In a study conducted a few years ago, a group of students were compared against a group of pensioners to see who were the better at remembering to fulfil a series of appointments and carry out a series of tasks. The result was that the pensioners consistently performed better at these memory tasks. Why? Because they were far better organised. They had developed skills in diary-keeping and checking, and in prioritising, which the students had yet to develop.

Imagine yourself going to retrieve a book from your shelves, a two-inch nail from your garden shed, or a particular t-shirt from your drawers. That task can be trivial, taking a couple of seconds, or it can be frustrating five-minute search. Your ability to retrieve is almost entirely dependent on how logically you stored the item in the first place. What holds for items around the house also holds for items to store in the brain: a logical approach to committing things to memory can be the difference between rapid, effortless recall and a frustrating and sometimes fruitless mind search.

Categorising before you store

Below is a list of sixteen cities on the American continent. Give yourself a minute to try to memorise the list:

Brasilia
Quebec

San Francisco
Tulsa
Newark
Pasadena
San Diego
New Orleans
Buenos Aires
Ottawa
Boston
Toronto
Rio de Janeiro
Sao Paolo
Tucson
New York

How did you do? A score of ten or more would be impressive in the time you were given, especially if you tried to remember the list in order. Of course the list as it stood had no structure to it. Trying to memorise and later retrieve it in that order is like a juggler trying to start his routine by members of the audience randomly throwing balls in his direction. It is possible, but hard work.

The most efficient way to commit a set of information to memory is usually to sort those items into some sort of logical order or set of categories first. A jumbled list is harder to make sense of than one that has logic to it. There are lots of different ways you could have categorised the list of cities, of which the most obvious is by geography:

Canada:	Toronto, Quebec, Ottawa
California:	San Jose, San Francisco, Pasadena
South America:	Brasilia, Sao Paolo, Buenos Aires, Rio de Janeiro
North East USA:	New York, Newark, Boston,
Southern USA:	Tulsa, Tucson, New Orleans

Once you have remembered one of the categories, the members of that category drop out more easily.

But you don't have to categorise cities by geography. There are many other ways in which a group like this can be categorised, for example by letter patterns. In this case, the sixteen fit rather neatly into five categories:

Table 3: Categories by letter pattern

The Sans and Saos	The News	The Ts	The Bs	OPQR
Sao Paolo	New Orleans	Toronto	Brasilia	Ottawa
San Jose	New York	Tulsa	Buenos Aires	Pasadena
San Francisco	Newark	Tucson	Boston	Quebec
				Rio

Or you could do something more eccentric and personal. Several of the cities feature in songs, so you could group those together with a little medley:

> *Jo Jo left his home in Tucson Arizona ... Twenty-four hours from Tulsa ... Deep down in Louisiana close to New Orleans ... I want to be a part of it, New York New York.*

Or whatever!

What applies to remembering a list of cities is just as important when it comes to remembering foreign vocabulary, historical information, or anything else you need to commit to memory. Organising into logical categories can significantly boost your ability to remember.

Brain-mapping

One way of organising information is to present it in the form of a brain map. (This concept was popularised in the 1960s by Tony Buzan, and is best known by the registered trademark Mindmap®.) The brain doesn't work in lists; it works by associations, with every piece of information linked with other pieces. A brain map transfers this web-like organisation of material onto the page.

For example, Diagram 3 is a simple brain map that I used in preparing a draft of this section of the book:

Diagram 3: A brain map

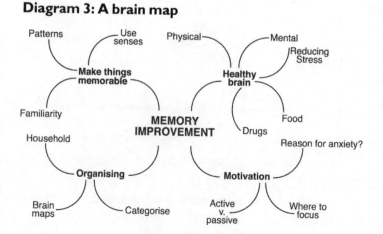

Starting with the subject in the middle of the page, the connected ideas and sub-headings branch out to form a network of ideas. Each branch represents a different topic.

Unlike a list, where you feel obliged to add items one after the other down the page, a brain map allows you to dot around the page as ideas occur to you. Each item at the end of a branch will prompt you to think of other, related items. If you get stuck, you can move to another branch and start adding there.

This is a quick and effective method of arranging information in an organised way, and even without illustrations, it is more memorable than a straight list. Typically my first stab at a brain-map is a mess, full of crossings-out and arrows to move things around, but it doesn't take long to make a neat copy.

I use these diagrams all the time, particularly as notes if I'm going to give a talk. If you think of the diagram like a clock, I put the subject in the centre, the introduction points of the talk at one o'clock, and then work around clockwise until the finish of the talk just before midnight.

Remembering where you left something

One of the commonest complaints about memory is being unable to find something that you've put down (glasses, a book, car keys and so on). Though there are other ways to reduce your forgetfulness for items around the house, the most effective is to organise and plan so that the problem doesn't arise in the first place.

Below are a few tips acquired from personal experience and from other people with similar problems. Some are straightforward, and what Basil Fawlty might describe as 'the bleedin' obvious'. Others involve a little more lateral thinking.

Books

If you can never find a book when you want it, there is a simple solution – do what libraries do, and arrange your assorted collection into categories. Have a section for biographies, another for thrillers, another for reference. Once you've done this major sort-through once, finding that book that you haven't seen for ages becomes far more straightforward, so long as you make a habit of putting it back in the right section. If you prefer your books to be arranged in a more aesthetically pleasing way, you could do what one person I know does, which is arrange the books by size, going from small ones on the left to the tallest on the right. Or you can arrange them by colour, so that all the green spines are grouped together separately from all the orange spines. If colours are your thing, you might find this just as easy a way of organising for easy retrieval as any other. It's a lot prettier, too.

Keys

Small objects like keys are prime candidates for getting

lost, and there are so many to lose, too. There are two common scenarios for losing items like keys. The first is that you put them down in an unfamiliar place while preoccupied with some other activity; the other is that you haven't used the key in question for months or even years, and you have quite forgotten where you put it after you last used it.

The obvious solution to the first problem is not to put the keys down in an unfamiliar location to start with. If you can train yourself to feel guilty whenever you put a key down other than in its 'home' you shouldn't fall into the sloppy habit in the first place. (<u>Memo to self</u>: must follow my own advice here, I'm notorious for lazily dropping things any old place and being distracted by something else.)

The best solution to the long-term key-losing problem is to keep all your keys together in a single, memorable place (when you aren't carrying them with you, that is). Perhaps it's a good idea not to make this central key store the shelf by the front door, since that is rather an invitation to prospective burglars. Why not choose somewhere a little more discreet like the inside of one of the food cupboards, for example? A couple of pensioners I interviewed recommended keeping the keys on separate hooks at eye level where they are clearly visible. By giving each key its own hook, you will quickly spot if any of the hooks are unoccupied. As icing on the cake, you can give each hook a clear label so that you don't have to remember which similar looking Yale key opens which door. Needless to say, you don't have to be elderly and short-sighted to benefit from this simple method.

Expensive items like spectacles

There are some items that you carry with you that you do sometimes have to put down in different places, and are therefore the most vulnerable to being forgotten. If the items are really valuable, such as an expensive special pair of spectacles, then this becomes a serious matter. On my recent holiday, I counted no fewer than four occasions when I left my treasured sunglasses somewhere and couldn't find them, only for them to eventually be tracked down. One of these days I'm going to lose them for good.

So what is the solution to this spectacle problem? There are a few options. If you're worried about losing something valuable, why not replace it with a cheaper version that you are prepared to lose instead? I adopted this tactic for a while, by buying a cheaper pair of sun specs for everyday use and only using the flash pair for special occasions. Sadly, I have lost the everyday pair, though perhaps this inadvertently demonstrates the effectiveness of the technique.

I read of an elderly chap who adopted a different tactic. He became so frustrated at losing his glasses (not helped by his poor eyesight) that he took to carrying an orange bag around with him. Whenever he put down his glasses he put them in the orange bag. He hasn't lost them since. I'm not sure it would be the solution in my case. If the purpose of trendy sunglasses is to create some semblance of a cool image, this would, I fear, be completely negated if I start putting them in an orange bag …

Pens and other cheap items

For cheaper items like pens and paper clips there is a different strategy you could adopt, namely the safety-in-numbers technique. If you are prone to losing pens, then why not just buy vast numbers of them. You can get a box of 100 cheap biros for a few pounds. Every time you lose one, all you have to do is go to the box to get another. After a while, your lost pens will start surfacing all over the house – behind sofas, on bookshelves and so on – so you will always have a pen close at hand. You will also begin to discover certain places where pens tend to end up. (In my case it's the glove box of the car, which has now become a reliable place to go if I can't find something to write with.) You may think this strategy sounds off the wall, but I met one person who swears by it! And if you are worried that the blitz approach is environmentally wasteful, reassure yourself that somebody somewhere will find your pen and will put it to good use, in the same way that the free newspapers handed out at railway stations are happily left on seats only to be picked up and read by the next passenger to sit there.

In all of these things, organisation is the key. Set up systems that will make recalling previously stored information as straightforward as possible or will reduce the chance of you forgetting or mislaying things that you need.

Organising for disorganised people

I must confess that of all the vital areas of memory improvement, organisation of information is the one with which I have the greatest difficulty. If you could see my desk at the moment, you'd know what I meant.

I'm reassured by those who say that chaotic people create their own sort of organisation, in which the stuff that is nearest to hand is the stuff that is likely to be of greatest use (thus if you've forgotten where you put something, look in the immediate vicinity first). I'm also reassured by those who say that as long as you retain a sense of humour, you can live even in the most outrageous chaos. I particularly like the notion that in the constant search for items that you have forgotten, you benefit from the serendipity of happening upon things that you weren't looking for but you are delighted to rediscover.

Still, disorganisation is a nuisance and a time-waster for everyone. A clear desk and an organised method of categorising information are vital aids to reducing incidents of forgetfulness. I would recommend that whatever it is you think you might end up losing or for-getting, start organising for it now. Set up those key hooks, create that drawer in your filing cabinet labelled 'IDs and passports', buy that little booklet to sit by the bed where you can jot those elusive thoughts that occur to you at midnight. Do it today. When you have to look for those items next year, you will be grateful to yourself for your forward planning.

If organising is not your style, you can do a lot worse than find somebody organised whom you can hire to give your affairs a regular blitz. If you are lucky enough to have a partner for whom organising comes naturally, better still.

8
Making Things More Memorable

Topics covered

- Using your senses
- Looking for patterns
- Making the unfamiliar familiar

In Chapter 4, I used the crude analogy of a faulty video recorder to explain why we can sometimes fail to remember things. The first item on the list was having a faulty RECORD button. If you don't store it, you can't retrieve it. This chapter is about ways to improve the quality of recordings, so that what you try to retrieve later on is likely to be more accurate and better quality.

Using your senses

In one of the earliest and most famous studies of memory, the Victorian scientist Sir Francis Galton wrote to a group of his learned colleagues to ask them to recall in as much detail as they could an image of what they had had for breakfast that morning. He found that most of them were able to remember what they had for breakfast, but also that their visual recollections varied enormously. Some simply remembered they had eaten eggs and rolls with marmalade without any image coming to mind, while others saw vivid colour images of the whole experience, including the flowers on the plates and the people sat at the table.

This story illustrates two things: that people remember things in different ways, and also that the senses can play an important part in the memory. In fact all of us hold memories derived from each of our senses. You can check this out by trying the following (after reading the instruction, you might need to close your eyes to get the full effect):

- Picture a horse walking down your street, and listen out for the sounds it makes.
- Think of bacon frying on a saucepan. Can you see it bubbling? Can you hear it? Can you smell it?
- Imagine eating a 99 ice cream. Can you feel the chocolate flake crumbling in your mouth? Can you feel texture of the ice cream as you lick it, and the cold sensation on your teeth?

You were probably able to conjure up at least one of the senses here, maybe all of them, though depending on the way your brain works the different senses will be stronger or weaker. Of all the senses, it is visual recall that is strongest for most people, followed by sound and touch. (It is claimed that more than half the population picture things when they are remembering them.) Curiously, smells can be quite difficult to recall, yet when you are exposed to them they can be one of the most powerful cues for bringing associated memories back.

Knowing your sensual preference for learning is an important step in improving your ability to remember. After all, if you are a mainly a visual person, then listening to a list of words being read out is not the most helpful way of committing that information to memory.

Picturing a Shopping List

Last week, I went to the local supermarket with my wife, who had the master shopping list written down. As is our normal practice, she had control of the cart while I went on forays to pick up batches of four items from the list, which of course required me to remember what the four items were. Having struggled to recall all the items in one such batch of four, I decided for the next one to create an image that combined all four of the items.

I now realise that I can still remember three of those four items – eggs, milk and strawberry jam (I pictured eggs and milk beaten together to form scrambled egg, into which was dolloped some strawberry jam and whatever the other thing was). I think this is noteworthy – not that I have forgotten one of the four items, but that three of them have stuck. There is of course no particular reason why I should have retained any of the items on that shopping list, but the visual image of the scrambled egg and jam was a powerful one that lodged in my memory and is still there a week later. The rest of the shopping list has vanished from my memory.

The egg, milk and jam image stuck with me because I have a tendency towards visual memory. Your own preferred way of remembering may be through the sound of the words – for example the rhythm – or it may simply be that the sequence egg-milk-jam registers with you as a pattern without any apparent connection to your senses at all. As one woman commented to me: 'When I see a list like that, it just "sticks", I don't know why.' (I can suggest one reason why the list might stick with her. She is a keen cook, so much of her life revolves around ingredients. Any new information about this topic therefore naturally links to the many thoughts already fixed in her memory.)

The principle of using the senses can apply to anything you want to remember. If you leave a package some-where – on the kitchen table, say – and want to be confident that you will quickly find it again, don't just picture the place where you have left it, but listen to the sound as it drops onto the table, say out loud the words 'package-kitchen', even make a note of what it feels like reaching over and placing the package down. The more of the associated visual setting, sounds and smells that you can link to the thing you want to remember, the more cues you have to bring those memories back later.

You could try to make every single act into a deliberate, memorable process, but that would be overkill. Instead you should concentrate your efforts on those items that it is vital for you to remember, or which you know you have a history of mislaying. One practical strategy would be to choose one object – your keys say – and make a sense-laden record every time you put them down. If it works, and becomes a comfortable habit, you can push the boat out and start doing it for, let's say, your passport.

Looking for patterns

How easy do you find it to remember this list of symbols in sequence?

At first glance it doesn't look memorable at all, it is just a series of shapes. Some of the symbols look like letters and numbers. If you use a bit of artistic licence, you can read the sequence as J U L 3 0 C 7 N R. This may help marginally, but even this sequence is not particularly memorable. It is an apparently random jumble of letters and digits, with no obvious hook to help you to store and retrieve it. Except … the first five symbols are J U L 3 0, which might make you think of the date July 30th. Maybe by repeatedly chanting something like 'July 30 See 7 N R' it would begin to stick, but I wouldn't bet on being able to remember that little phrase accurately in a week's time.

The fact is that unfamiliar patterns are difficult to remember, and one of the secrets to remembering things is to find in them something that connects to your previous experience and to patterns that you recognise.

Looking back at the sequence of symbols, can you spot anything else that might make it simpler and more recognisable? Try turning the page upside down. You'll discover that the sequence looks exactly the same when it is inverted! This is a huge help when trying to remember it. If you remember that the middle symbol is a square, the only challenge now is to memorise the first four symbols:

The last four are the same as the first four if you turn the page upside down. This has greatly simplified the task of memorising the sequence.

You may, however, have spotted an even more effective way of remembering the shapes. Below is a grid for a game of noughts and crosses, with each square numbered:

1	2	3
4	5	6
7	8	9

Look at the shapes of the grid in positions 1, 2, 3, 4 … and so on. These are exactly the same as the shapes in the earlier sequence in the correct order. Now you have learned that the noughts and crosses grid is the key to remembering the sequence of symbols, you will have no difficulty instantly reproducing the nine shapes in the correct order, and furthermore you will be able to accurately remember them in a week or even a month's time (should you feel the desire to do so.)

As a general rule, if you can spot simple, recognisable patterns, you will find things easier to remember.

A Memorable Pattern for Waitrose

In 2002, the Waitrose store launched a new home delivery service called Ocado. I heard an advertisement for it on the radio, and my first thought was, 'What an instantly forgettable name'. It seemed to be a meaningless and rather bland new word. If I was trying to recall it, I thought to myself, I could easily make the mistake of calling it Acoda, or Odaco, or Acado, or Ocodo, each of which is equally unmemorable.

I was about to record it as a good example of how to make something unmemorable, when it struck me that Ocado is the end of the word 'avocado'. Having made this link between avocado, the kind of posh food item you buy from Waitrose, and Ocado, I was unlikely to forget the name. When faced with a range of options I would now have no doubt about which was the correct one. I gave myself the credit for spotting this

Ocado–avocado connection, but I later read that the people responsible for inventing the new brand name chose Ocado because they thought it would bring associations of fresh avocados to customers, thus 'reinforcing the fresh quality that the Waitrose brand represents'. Well, I certainly fell for it!

Making the unfamiliar familiar

The earlier example of the sequence of shapes shows that a good memory isn't just about being able to absorb everything that's thrown at you. If you can link something apparently meaningless into something that is already familiar to you, memorising can turn from being almost impossible to being a piece of cake.

People often seem a little embarrassed to admit that the way they remember things is by linking them to something familiar. But we all do it at some time or another, because it's a natural way for our brains to work. Here are a few examples that people gave to me when researching this book.

When I'm setting out the coloured balls before snooker, I have difficulty remembering which order to place the green, brown and yellow. So I always say to myself 'Great Britain's Yellow' as a reminder of the right order (G, B, Y). On an old map of mine, Britain was shaded yellow so this is easy to remember.

When I'm shopping, I turn the list into a song to a well known tune, and sing it to myself. Like, recently

I used the tune of 'When I'm Sixty-Four' for my shopping list and it went something like: 'When I get shampoo, cleaning my hair, sausage chicken sprouts.' If anyone overhears me they must think I'm mad!

When I'm playing a tune on the piano that has the right hand playing two beats and the left hand three, I say to myself 'Nice cup of tea, nice cup of tea, nice cup of tea' to get the right rhythm.

And here's my favourite, from a friend of mine, Sara:

When I go into the kitchen to make coffee for friends who are over for dinner, I help myself to remember whose is which by linking the positions of the mugs to the politics of the guests. So I put the mug of the person who I think is the most left-wing on the left of the tray, the one who is most right-wing on the right of the tray, and work inwards from there. Of course I don't tell them this is what I'm doing.

I look forward to going round to dinner with Sara sometime just to see what she thinks my political leanings are!

Of course I'm not suggesting that you adopt the charmingly quirky approaches that these people used, though of course there may be an idea there that takes your fancy. The point is that these personal memory aids work because they link the item to be remembered to something that is familiar to the person doing the remembering.

9
Strategies for Better Retrieving

Topics covered

- Practice
- Getting a cue
- Systematic searching

We become aware that our memory has failed only when it comes to retrieving the information that we know we once knew. Sometimes failure to retrieve a memory is because the information is (as far as we can tell) irretrievably lost, perhaps because we never stored it properly in the first place. Just as often, the problem is finding the route back to a memory you know is in there.

You will find it far easier to retrieve information if you followed the advice in the previous two chapters, storing it in an organised way and making it more memorable. Even so, spontaneous recall of information is not always easy, but there are three ways that you can help yourself:

Practice

Before you have to remember something 'for real', it helps to practice. Practice means trying to repeat back what you are seeking to commit to memory, and checking how well you are doing.

Repetition is one of the ways in which information is transferred from short-term memory to long-term memory. It serves two purposes. Not only does it help to etch the information into your memory in the first place, but if you repeat back without any prompts, you are also forcing yourself to establish retrieval routes – routes that you will be able to reuse later when it comes to recalling the information at will.

Some forms of repetition are better than others. Reading something and then reading it again gives you little feedback on what has or has not sunk in. On the other hand, reading something and testing yourself on it with the book closed – or even better, getting somebody else to test you – quickly exposes what you don't know, and helps to set the foundations for your future retrieval paths.

Trying to repeat back information unprompted is a good discipline whatever it is you are trying to remember. When you meet somebody for the first time, repeat their name when they are introduced. When you finish a chapter whose contents you want to remember, close the book and try to recall the main points. When you hear a joke that you like, find an opportunity to repeat it to somebody as soon as possible (or if you don't have an audience, make a note of it and then test yourself on it later).

It helps the process of remembering if the thing you are repeating back means something to you, but old-fashioned 'learning by rote' can be just as effective if you repeat something often enough. For example, if you remember the meaningless word 'Supercalifragi- listicexpialidocious' from the film *Mary Poppins*, it is almost certainly because you listened to it and repeated it back many times.

In the same way, if you say 'Seven eights are fifty-six' often enough (however deeply or shallowly you under- stand its meaning) then if somebody says 'Seven eights' to you, you can't help but finish it off with 'Fifty-six'.

The most effective way to commit something to your long term memory is to test yourself on it frequently at first, but to decrease the frequency as time goes on. One such strategy goes like this:

Test your recall
1. Immediately
2. Then ten minutes later
3. An hour later
4. Several hours later
5. The next day
6. The next week
7. The next month ... and so on.

Note how the interval between each attempted recall of the information increases about fivefold each time. Each time you recall, check your accuracy and put right any mistakes you made (if the same mistake arises sev- eral times, you should look for a different, richer way of committing it to memory).

This approach, or others like it, will steadily help to commit the information to memory, so that after a while it will become part of your mental furniture.

Rote-learning for Life

Richard gave me this example of how rote-learning has stuck with him all his life.

At school, in the 1970s, I chose to study German (mainly as I recall because it meant I could avoid biology, where there was compulsory dissection of frogs). German is a very structured and logical language, but one of its more arbitrary, illogical aspects is in its use of prepositions – on, under, with, through and so on. In English, it doesn't matter which preposition you use, the pronoun 'the' never changes. So we say 'without the mouse', 'under the mouse', 'with the mouse' and so on. However, in German, the pronoun changes depending on the preposition you use. 'Without the mouse' is 'ohne die Maus' but 'with the mouse' is 'mit der Maus'.

Remembering which German preposition does what could have been a real bind had our teacher not drilled into us the rule for which prepositions do what. For the prepositions that take the accusative he had us repeat the phrase 'durch fur gegen ohne um wider' in a slightly warlike chant until we had learned it by heart (we were all about fourteen, and seemed to have a good laugh when we did it). For those prepositions that take the dative we learned 'aus ausser bei, mit nach seit von zu', the last five words being said very quickly.

> *In the early stages we were learning this chant without knowing what most of the words meant (I'm still struggling to recall what 'wider' means) but that didn't stop this being a very useful check back when I needed to use one of the other prepositions in a sentence. The proof of the pudding is that these preposition checks are still with me now, and on those very rare occasions where I have to speak German, I make use of them.*

Getting a cue

Having fixed a memory by learning and repetition (you hope!), the moment will finally come when you are called on to retrieve the information. Bumping into an old friend on the street, talking about that film that starred Humphrey Bogart … these are the moments when your ability to recall information will be truly tested.

Fortunately, you don't have to rely just on recalling the information itself. The sounds, smells and visual surroundings that you were exposed to when you first learned the information can provide vital cues to link back to the thing you are trying to remember.

Sometimes the cue effect can happen unexpectedly. I asked an actress who has to remember long passages of text about her experiences of forgetting lines. She told me that she often has a moment of panic in the wings when her mind goes blank and she can't think of her first line. Yet as soon as she goes on stage and is surrounded by the props and atmosphere in which she learned the lines, they come flooding back. The secret of recalling information can be location, location, location.

Something similar happens in examinations. Pupils at Jenny's school always sat in the same positions in class. When it came to public examinations, her teacher always made sure that the children sat in their normal positions because the familiar seating position would aid recall.

It is not only location that can help to trigger memories. For example, if you were drinking coffee when you stored the information, the smell of coffee can help to trigger those memories later on.

You can exploit this principle even when you aren't able to perform on the same stage or sit in the same position for an exam. By deliberately surrounding yourself with certain objects and smells (a lucky mascot and some lavender, for example) you can improve your recall in an examination simply by placing the mascot and lavender in front of you.

Performing on stage or taking an exam are examples of planned occasions when you know you will be required to recall particular information. What about those random life situations where you can't be sure what sort of things you will have to retrieve? The mascot-and-lavender tactic (as we might call it) won't help here. It would be impractical, to say the least, to waft lavender under your nose when being introduced to Angie Smith and then to carry lavender around with you on the off-chance that you might bump into her again one day.

If the cues aren't there waiting for you, then you need to go looking for them. If you can't retrieve exactly what you want, try to retrieve anything you know that is vaguely relevant. Meandering around the subject can lead to an unexpected cue. I used to use this tactic when trying to answer Trivial Pursuit questions. I remember on one occasion being asked the following question during one game: 'Which mountain range runs the entire length of the Italian peninsula?' I couldn't think of the answer, so I thought aloud about anything I knew about Italy and mountains. The word 'Pennines' randomly popped up, which led to the Aha! moment when I recalled the Italian Apennines (and won my piece of cheese).

Another way to stimulate recall is by reliving an experience. Crime investigators use such techniques to coax more details out of witnesses to crimes. One is to ask the witness to imagine herself back at the crime scene, but to place herself in the position of one of the other participants. 'Suppose you were the man you saw with the dog. What was going on around you?' You can even ask the witness to replay the events backwards. Instead of asking 'What happened first?', you ask 'What happened last?' These jolts to the memory can help find links that are being missed if the witness simply replays the story that they have told several times before.

And if it works for witnesses, maybe it could work

for you in that quest to find the missing keys. The obvious route is to retrace your steps, thinking of all the rooms you have visited. But you might also take a more lateral route, for example by asking yourself what you were talking about when you first entered the house (which might prompt the thought that: 'We were debating whether or not Charing Cross underground station is on the Jubilee Line, so I went to find an A to Z, and … put the keys down!')

Cues aren't just a part of deliberate recall, they also lead to spontaneous recall of events you weren't even trying to remember. Walking into an old church or a school playground can bring back vivid memories of experiences that you had there as a child, which you thought you had forgotten. The novelist Marcel Proust based an entire novel on the memories triggered by the smell of madeleine cakes.

When Did the Statue Topple?

During the Iraq war, there was a famous moment when Saddam Hussein's statue was pulled down by ropes attached to an American vehicle. But what was the date? I have no cue that directly links it to a particular date, but I have a series of associations that can get me close. I remember that I was in a hotel in Jersey at the time (a classic case of flashbulb memory that I'm prepared to trust). *Why?* The reason why I was in Jersey was that I was giving a joint talk with somebody. *What do I know about him?* The man I was giving a talk with was only able to be there because he worked at a school and it was his Easter holiday, so it must have been late March or April. *Anything else?* We had our baby daughter with us. She was born on 5 March, and we weren't allowed to take her on an aeroplane until she was at least four weeks old. So that meant the Jersey event was April at the earliest. *And so ...* Saddam's statue must have been pulled down in April 2003. Elementary, my dear Watson! (Alas, I don't have any cues that are precise enough to identify the day, though I'd hazard a guess at around 10 April. I'm not going to cheat and look it up).

Systematic retrieval

Chapter 7 talked about the importance of being systematic and organised to help you to memorise something. The same principle applies when it comes to recall.

Systematic retrieval is particularly suited to overcoming the tip-of-tongue moment where you can't recall a word. Starting at A, go through the alphabet a letter at a time. Once you hit upon the letter that starts the word, that is likely provide the cue to trigger the whole thing. It can help to do this out loud, making various sounds with each letter so that you can tap into your auditory memory: 'Ay ... Ah ... At ... Be ... Ba ... Bo ... Co ... Ca ... that's it, *Casablanca*!'

When it comes to remembering a list of items, a systematic approach helps to ensure that you don't forget anything. One occasion where you may need to think of a list comes when you are packing for holiday. The unsystematic approach is simply to pack items as you think of them (shirt, toothbrush, camera, socks). For me, such an approach is destined to lead to some item being left behind.

The more thorough approach is to work by categories, and then to go methodically through each one. There are lots of ways of categorising items to make sure you are thorough in packing everything. For example, you might categorise clothes as hot weather/cold weather, or indoor/outdoor. To ensure you forget nothing, it pays to have more than one set of categories. So you might, for example, start by methodically going from toes to head (socks, shoes, trousers … etc) and then crosscheck by doing the same check again for formal wear and then informal wear.

I suspect that most of us rely on our brains alone to think of what items to pack, but of course this is an ideal occasion for making use of pen and paper. Many people are keen on lists, but a more effective way of jotting down information that has different headings is to use the brain maps described on page 97.

Part Three:

How to Remember Particular Things

10
How to Remember Names

Topics covered

- Why names can be hard to recall
- Register the name at the start
- Make associations with the name
- Rehearse
- Play for time
- The avoidance strategy
- Make it easier for others

Of all the areas of memory that cause people anxiety or frustration, names come at the top of the list.

'What's in a name?' asked Juliet from her balcony in Shakespeare's most famous scene. 'That which we call a rose by any other name would smell as sweet.'

A rose might indeed smell as sweet by any other name, but Romeo was given one name and no other, and if Juliet had inadvertently called him Timothy or Albert, or simply said 'I'm terribly sorry, what was it again?' their budding romance might have been nipped then and there. A Romeo by any other name just will not do.

It isn't only people's names that get forgotten. We forget names of chemicals or the names of films too. But the impact of forgetting a person's name is far greater because of the embarrassment that it can cause, not only for the person who forgets it but also for the person whose name is forgotten. Curiously, if you forget somebody's name you blame your memory, but if somebody forgets your name, you are more likely to assume that this is because you are not important enough to have made an impression. The truth is, of course, that name aberrations crop up frequently even for those people you know well.

Why names can be hard to recall

People find it odd that they remember somebody's face but not their name. In fact there is nothing odd about this at all if you think about many of the situations where this problem arises. When you bump into somebody and remember their face but not their name you are using two completely separate processes.

- For the face, you are using *recognition*.
- For the name, you are using *recall*.

Recognition is almost always much easier than recall. Just think about those tests you used to take at school. If you couldn't quite remember an answer, a multiple choice question was enough to prompt you in the right direction (testing your recognition powers). But those questions that offered you no options to choose from were testing your powers of recall, and were considerably more difficult.

For a fair comparison of your ability to remember names and faces, you should test them the other way round. If you are shown a list of names of people that you know, are you able to picture all of their faces? In fact it isn't that easy, and of course this is the exact equivalent of being presented with a series of faces and then trying to recall the names. If people you bumped into wore t-shirts listing four choices for you to select from, you'd have little difficulty correctly recalling their names!

There is, however, another factor that helps to explain why names of people are more forgettable than, say, the name of a tool. Let's imagine you know somebody called Anne. One reason why there could be a problem remembering her name is that you no doubt know several people called Anne. Other than their name and their gender, these people are unlikely to have much in common. There is nothing about the group of people called 'Anne' that particularly distinguishes them from the group of people called 'Jane' or 'Rachel' or 'Debbie', so when you meet this particular Anne, there are no cues from her appearance that tell you she's any more likely to be an 'Anne' than a 'Jane'.

This is very different from the group of objects called 'spanner' for example. Like 'Annes', spanners can look very different from each other, but unlike 'Annes', they all have certain properties in common, such as being metal and having a long handle and 'jaws'. These features make them unambiguously spanners rather than, for example, saws. So one of the problems in retrieving personal names is that they are arbitrary labels for objects with which they have no particular connection. (There are exceptions of course – I knew of a girl called Hazel who happened to have hazel eyes, and needless to say her name was easy to recall.)

There are tactics and techniques one can adopt for avoiding these awful name gaffes.

Register the name at the start

The problem with names begins when you are first exposed to them. Often you might first meet somebody at a function of some kind where there is lots of background noise and distraction. Not a good start. Introductions are often made in groups, too.

'This is Sally.'

'Hello!'

'And Jonathan.'

'Hi!'

'And Barbara.'

'Pleased to meet you …'

By the time it has reached three, you will already be struggling to hold all of these new names. And when it's one of those inundations of names at a dinner party where you arrive late and ten names get hurled at you, you might as well (literally) forget it!

Even if the introduction is to just one person, the tendency is for you not to be concentrating when you first hear the name. Check your own behaviour next time you meet somebody new. Maybe you are a little anxious. You might be thinking about all sorts of social niceties like making sure you have eye contact and that you look your best, planning what you are going to say next, and perhaps building up to the moment where you give your own name to them in a clear, audible fashion. All of these things are distractions, which mean that when somebody gives you their name, you are not concentrating on it. No wonder that within seconds you have forgotten it.

The golden rule of name-storing is to repeat back the name of the person who just said 'hello' to you as quickly as possible.

'The name's Bob.'

'Hello, Bob.'

This comes as second nature to a salesman, and should really be second nature to anybody. As mentioned in Chapter 9, repetition is one of the most effective ways of putting a trace into your memory. In this case it also has the added advantage of ensuring that you correctly heard the name in the first place.

'The name's Barry.'

'Hello, Gary.'

'No, Barry.'

This might cause a moment of embarrassment, but a stitch in time saves nine, and the embarrassment of making this mistake later in the conversation is considerably higher.

You can extend the repetition rule by ensuring that you fill your conversation with the person's name. 'Well, Bob, I used to work for Quibbles Machine

Company ...' 'So tell me, Bob, how long would you say it takes to thaw a frozen chicken?'

Many people do this, either as a deliberate ploy to fix names or just as a habit they have grown into. On the one hand it helps to keep names fresh, but on the other, the listener can find it irritatingly 'chummy'. Thinking about my own behaviour in conversations, I would say that I practically *never* use people's first names, unless I am calling out to them, saying hello to them, or introducing them to somebody else. I am probably among the majority of British people in this regard. Does this make us collectively worse at remembering names? The answer is probably 'yes'.

One of the best ways of getting somebody's name is to ask them for a card. Again, this is standard practice in business circles, but as we increasingly become individuals with portfolio lifestyles and CVs, carrying a card is becoming more commonplace even for those people not working for an organisation. Once you have somebody's card, one little trick to enhance your memory of the person is to write something about them (their interests? where you met them?) on the back of the card when you get home. The very act of recording this information helps to etch the memory of the person more firmly in your mind, even if you never refer to their card again. Of course, this also opens up the possibility of you creating a filing system. It depends how far you want to go.

Make associations with the name

One approach often promoted in memory improvement is to use association to help to fix a name. The idea is to link the person's name with some physical feature that they have so that the next time you see them, the physical feature links back to the name. For example, if Carol has a particularly prominent nose, you can imagine her nose as an organ playing the introduction to a Christmas carol (how about 'Rudolf the Red-nosed Reindeer'?). Alternatively you can make a rhyme to help a name to stick. Say to yourself 'Hannah likes to play the pianna' (it helps if she really *does* play the piano!).

I do occasionally use this sort of device, if it occurs to me to do so in the turmoil of all the introductions that are going on. I find that it can certainly help in the short term (the duration of a meal, for example), but unless I make a point of rehearsing the link later on, the memory fades quite quickly. So if you are like me, you should think of this as a useful short-term tactic.

Some memory performers advocate taking the approach a lot further. They take each first name, and associate an image with that name. For example, Helen sounds a bit like Hall, so Hall becomes the code word for Helen. When you meet somebody called Helen, you then pick out a prominent feature, her high forehead for example, and create an image linking the forehead to some hall, maybe a hall whose cavernous arches are the same shape as the forehead. Next time you meet

Helen, you see her forehead, which reminds you of the cavernous arches in your keyword, Hall, and Hall triggers you to think of Helen. Got it?

Most people offer two major criticisms of this technique. One is that it requires quite a lot of effort to learn it, not least because in order to remember a name, you are having to remember a link as well. Advocates of such techniques say that it is worth the investment of time, but the comment I get back from people who might benefit from using it is almost always: 'I really couldn't be bothered!' And there is another, even more damning, criticism. Sometimes the associations formed in this way can lead to confusion down the line unless the association is clear and unambiguous. Robert becomes Robber, but when recalling a robber you are in danger of thinking of the word 'Nick'.

Winston told me how just such an error once caused him huge embarrassment.

> *I was at a function and met somebody with the surname Burke. Next time I met him, I confidently shook him by the hand and said 'It's Pratt, isn't it?'*

Rehearsal

A tennis player about to embark on a serious game always warms up first. You can do the same thing when it comes to using names, by rehearsing them in advance.

Name slips can happen even in the most planned of circumstances. Tom explains:

> *I vividly recall an occasion in my mid-twenties when I invited three acquaintances around for dinner. They didn't know each other, so when they had arrived, it was my job to do the introductions. 'This is Anna, this is Kate, and this is ...' and my mind went blank. The male in front of me was a long-standing friend, yet I couldn't for the life of me remember his name. It was acutely embarrassing for all concerned when Jon was forced to introduce himself. Ever since then I have sworn by the strategy of name rehearsal, particular if it is an event where you know who is going to be attending.*

Giving yourself a few moments in advance to recall the names of familiar people can be invaluable preparation. Retrieving a name can sometimes take a few seconds, but once you have done it once, the next time you try to retrieve it you should find that it comes back almost instantaneously. Once the memory trace has been activated, it stays 'warm' for some time.

I can give an example of reactivating a memory trace that happened to me the day before I wrote this section. I was trying to think of the name of the English actor who appeared in *Raiders of the Lost Ark* and *A Room with a View*. It was a tip-of-the-tongue moment, as I knew he had a slightly unusual name and I could picture his face, but I had to go through the alphabet to find the trigger that brought back his name – Denholm Elliott.

It was a name I probably hadn't thought of for a couple of years. Today, trying to think of the name again, it came back instantly. A small amount of practice can have a huge impact on recall.

Play for time

The fact that names will come back with a little thought means that the tactic of playing for time can give you the vital seconds that you need in which to bring the name back. Instead of coming clean and admitting you can't remember the name right at the start, you can play the less awkward but more risky game of delay – especially if there is no immediate need to introduce this person to someone else.

Fortunately, while the name is often elusive, other information about the person does usually come to mind. You might remember their job or where you first met. It often pays simply to launch into conversation about the things you do know about this person. This conversation is likely to throw out cues, one of which might be just the trigger you need to retrieve the name. Or, while nodding as you pretend to listen to your friend's chat, you can be quietly working your way through the alphabet in the hope of finding the right cue letter.

I've heard of other more drastic tactics that helped a person to play for time while appearing to be fully in control. For example, as you enter conversation and realise that you don't know the name, you suddenly 'remember' that you have left something important in your coat pocket and need to retrieve it, but will be back in a second. That buys you time to think, or even, in more drastic circumstances, to make that rapid phone call to a friend to ask them what *is* the name of the man who is head of the department.

One man I spoke to, Peter, told me of his delaying tactic.

> *When I go into the local town, I invariably bump into people who used to work at my factory. If I need to remember their name, one device I use is to ask them a question like 'Have you seen any of the lads from the workshop recently?' This usually sets them off reminiscing, and in the middle of one of their stories they will often throw in a line like: 'And he said to me, "Stan" he said, "It's never been the same since you left."' Which of course tells me that I'm talking to Stan!*

It is, however, possible to become paranoid about forgetting names, and cause yourself unnecessary anxiety in the process. Paul gave me the following example:

> *I have clients who ring me up to ask how a project is progressing, and I've been known to forget who the client is. I had one caller who said, 'Hi, Fred here, how's it going?'*
>
> *I was at a total loss to know which client it was and what sort of information he would be after. So I said, 'I'm fine, how about you?' hoping he would say something to jog my memory.*

But unhelpfully he replied, 'Oh fine, same as ever.'

So I fished a bit further and said 'I'm sure last time we spoke you were going to go into a new field or take on an extra responsibility, so what are you doing now?'

And he said, 'Oh, still the same, life insurance and pensions.'

At which point the penny dropped. This guy was a complete stranger, trying to flog me a pension!

The avoidance strategy

The most risky device of all when it comes to names is to avoid them altogether – risky because if you get found out, your credibility can suffer badly, unless you confess all. Film director Richard Attenborough famously confessed that because he was so hopeless with names he would always refer to people he met as 'darling'. At least he was honest about it. And one designer I spoke to told me that at an office where he worked, all the men used to refer to each other as 'Bill'. That way, they never had any difficulty over names.

'Morning, Bill, how are you?'

'Oh, not so bad, Bill, and yourself?'

Other avoidance strategies are more subtle. One is to make sure that you never take a partner to any function, or if you do, make sure you split up. Introducing partners is the most common situation where names can escape you, so by cutting out the source of the problem you can avoid it altogether. I knew somebody who made a point of doing this whenever it was possible!

Unfortunately, name introductions can be forced upon you without warning. Kay had an important job in PR and was therefore always at functions where she was meeting people. She told me about the following experience:

> I was at a launch party and spotted somebody I knew, but whose name I had forgotten. That was OK, because I was able to go up to her and catch up on things without any need to use her name. Unfortunately, somebody else who knew me, but not her, then approached us. I bluffed my way for a while, but things got desperate when a third guy walked up and said, 'Hi, Kay, how's it going?'
>
> I now had three people around me, none of whom knew each other, and none of whose names I could remember. It was awful. Fortunately they began introducing themselves to each other, which is just as well because I was rapidly running out of delaying tactics.

It reminds me of the episode of *Fawlty Towers* where Basil seeks to attract a better class of customer to his hotel by having a gourmet evening. Attempting to generate some small talk with the guests he starts to introduce one of the couples when he realises that he can't remember their names. In a final desperate bid to cover up for his mental block, Fawlty pretends to faint, at which point his guests finally introduce themselves to each other. There but for the grace of God …

Sometimes people try a bit of faking to get around

such problems. Mary confessed to me that she has often used a tactic of pretending to have remembered a name that she had actually forgotten. When introducing somebody, she would say up front, 'This is … I'm sorry, I have forgotten your name', at which point the person would reply, 'It's Janice' and Mary would say 'Oh I know it's *Janice*, it's your surname that has escaped me'. Such tactics can be useful as last resorts, though it can be hard to fake convincingly.

Beware, Faking it May Find You Out

I once attended a seminar being run by somebody who is prominent in the field of memory training. I chatted to him briefly after the seminar, and didn't meet him again until about five years later. I was introduced to him at an event where he was speaking, and reminded him that we had spoken briefly after one of his events a few years back. 'Hello, Rob,' he said, 'Yes, I thought I recognised you.'

I was flattered, and impressed. His remarkable powers of recall that showed how interested he must be in the people he meets. But something about his manner in our subsequent conversation made me suspicious. As chance would have it, the following year, we were both invited onto a radio programme together, and before the recording we had a cup of tea.

This time I didn't offer him any cues about us having met before. When he was introduced to me, his blank expression confirmed that he had no recollection of our two previous meetings.

Beware! Your sins will find you out.

Make it easier for others

I have always liked the so-called Golden Rule: 'Do unto others that which you would have them do unto you.' Nowhere does this seem to be more relevant than in the business of remembering people's names.

You know that the next time you bump into some-body you haven't seen for a while that there is a chance that they will have forgotten your name. So to save the all-round embarrassment, why not make it a habit to look for the signs, and help them out. If their body language suggests they are struggling to think of who you are, there are lots of ways to defuse the situation. One is simply to say, 'I'm Jenny Williams, we met at the conference last year'. Another is to feed plenty of cues about who you are so that you can engage in conver-sation and your name will occur to your colleague in the middle of it.

The most common situation where you may need to jump in and rescue a colleague is when they have some-body with them – which of course means they will feel obliged to introduce you both. Debrett's, the guide to etiquette, says that at the first sign of a hesitation when you are about to be introduced, it's your job to leap in and say, 'Hello, I'm Bob Smith'. This not only saves your friend the embarrassment of introducing you; it also means that the friend's colleague will probably now introduce themselves to you, thus saving your friend that introduction too. It's a double whammy!

Since somebody you meet for the first time is likely to have just the same problems as you have in registering your name in the first place, you can make it a habit of handing over a card when you introduce yourself. If this seems a bit formal, or indeed pushy, introduce yourself first, and then offer your card after a suitable few moments of conversation. Again, offering your card is likely to trigger a reciprocal offer, which gets both of you off the hook.

If you have a difficult name to remember, it might be worth devising a way to make it easier for people to get it right first time. My surname, Eastaway, is invariably misrecorded as 'Easterway' or 'Eastway'. I sometimes introduce myself as 'Eastaway – as in Castaway but with an E'. It works, as long as people know how to spell castaway!

How Kaffe Made a Name For Himself

The world-renowned quilt-maker Kaffe Fassett has a particularly hard name to remember. In a radio interview he explained how he had made his name more memorable. He started saying to his clients:

> *You have a safe asset*
> *with Kaffe Fassett*
>
> His catchphrase certainly worked for me. I'd never heard of him before that interview, and have never forgotten his name since. It was an ingenious means of combining a social courtesy with some self-promotion, what you might call enlightened self-interest.

11
How to Remember Numbers

Topics covered

- Important numbers to remember
- Short-term recall
- Patterns and chunking
- Association
- Turning numbers into words
- Orders of magnitude

Some people find numbers easy to remember. As one person commented to me:

> *I have no difficulty committing numbers to memory. Perhaps it's because I'm an accountant.*

Dennis reported that not long ago, the number 3826145 had suddenly popped back into his mind. It was the Co-op number that he had as a child. 'What's remarkable,' he commented, 'is that as far as I'm aware I did not think about this number for over 30 years, yet it suddenly came to me. I have no idea why.'

For others, however, numbers are an Achilles heel. 'I find numbers impossible to remember, I don't even bother to try,' said Robin. One mother remarked:

> *I can't even remember my children's mobile numbers, except for the last three digits. I think this is laziness on my part.*

What, then, are the tricks for recalling numbers, especially if you have no affinity with them?

Important numbers to remember

There are two different types of number that we encounter in managing our lives.

One type is a statistic or a measurement, such as the amount of money in your bank account or the weight of a bag of potatoes.

The other type of number acts as an identification or a label. Your customer ID, your security PIN, your car registration and your telephone number aren't counting anything, they are a convenient means of uniquely identifying you or your belongings, instead of using your name.

The difference between these two types of number is important, because while it is often acceptable to get a measuring number only *approximately* right, an ID has to be remembered perfectly or it is useless. Most of this chapter therefore concentrates on numbers that are used as labels, though a technique for remembering a telephone number can work just as well for remembering the date of the Battle of Trafalgar or the height of Mount Kilimanjaro.

Thanks to the invention of portable electronic aids,

there is far less need today than there used to be for remembering numbers. Telephone numbers are easily saved and retrieved on a mobile phone, and pocket organisers are there if you need to keep a record of your bank sort code number, your NI number, house numbers and the rest.

In fact, when it comes down to it there are very few numbers that people absolutely have to keep stored in their brains. The only numbers that you really shouldn't write down are security numbers such as your PIN code for getting cash from the bank. And even here people find ingenious ways of getting around their reluctance or inability to commit numbers to memory.

Ingrid keeps her PIN number on a piece of card in the same part of her wallet as her cashpoint card, but in a disguised form. The piece of paper says: 'Steven's phone: 83694026.' This isn't a genuine phone number, simply a means by which she can remind herself that 4026 – the last four digits – are her personal code.

However, relying entirely on writing numbers down can make you vulnerable in those situations where you have left your notebook behind or when your phone's battery is flat. In cases like these, effort invested in memorising phone numbers, padlock codes and the rest pays a dividend.

Short-term recall

Whether you are numerate or not, you might be surprised to learn that you probably have an innate ability to remember any number for a short period of time, as long as the number is not too long.

Picture the scene. It's pouring with rain, your car has run out of petrol and you have left your mobile phone at home. You don't have a pen and paper on you, but you need to be able to ring your friend who lives locally and who may be able to rescue you. You find a phone box, but realise that you've forgotten your friend's number. Never mind, you can call directory enquiries; 118 118 (now there's a number that's easy to remember – it helps that you saw the advertisement for it so many times). You get through to them, and they give you the telephone number, which is local:

7619036

Can you remember it? Read it aloud once more and then close your eyes and see if it has stuck. The chances are that you are able to recall this number accurately after repeating it just once, which means you can now hang up on the enquiry service and dial your friend.

This is your short-term, working memory in operation. The majority of adults find that they have little difficulty repeating back a seven-digit number that they have read or seen only once.

Suppose, however, that directory enquiries informed you that your friend's number is in fact:

735638429

Read it again, then test your ability to recall it.

You are doing well if you remembered that string of nine digits perfectly. Typically you will get the beginning and the end right, but mess up in the middle, maybe by transposing or omitting one of the digits.

As it happens, nine random digits are typically too many for the short-term memory to hold. Most people have an upper limit of seven, some can manage eight, and only very few can retain nine or more digits after one viewing (unless they are using other tricks that we will come on to later).

For many years, most phone numbers were no more than seven digits long, if you ignored the area code. Since that is the maximum length of number that people are comfortable remembering, the nation had little problem remembering phone numbers. These days the average phone number is longer, thanks mainly to the mobile phone numbers that typically start 07 followed by nine digits. This means we can no longer rely on parrot-like repetition and short-term memory.

To Remember Long Numbers, Learn Chinese!

The average number of digits that can be held in short-term memory depends on what language you speak. This is because what you are remembering is not the shape of the digits, but the sound that they make, and what determines the length of your short-term memory is the length of the sounds you are storing.

You remember the number 6 4 8 5 by the sounds 'Six four eight five'. In the Welsh language, the words used for different numbers are more complex. That same series of four digits would be remembered as 'Chwech pedwar ooeeth pimp', which takes longer to say. For this reason alone, short term memory in Welsh is only comfortable with six digits rather than the seven of the English Language. In contrast, Chinese words are much shorter sounds than English (*yi er san si wu liu qi*) so the upper digit span for Chinese people is ten. The moral is, if you want somebody to memorise a long telephone number, ask a Chinese speaker.

Patterns and chunking

The limit of seven digits applies only to numbers that have no obvious pattern to them. If you were faced with memorising a phone number such as:

987654321

you would have no difficulty memorising it instantly, because its pattern is so distinctive. You don't see nine separate digits, but rather a single pattern.

How about the following number?

132027344148

It probably looks a lot more random, unless you happen to spot that it is also based on a simple pattern:

$$13\ 20\ 27\ 34\ 41\ 48$$

Each pair of digits is seven larger than the previous pair.

By 'chunking' digits together in this way into familiar patterns, it is possible to quickly remember a number that is far more than seven digits long. Even chunking into unfamiliar patterns can help. You probably find 98275567 easier to remember if you pair up the digits: 98 27 55 67. The French always dictate telephone numbers as a series of two-digit numbers (ninety-eight, twenty-seven, fifty-five, sixty-seven), which suggests that they find this a more memorable way of storing a long sequence of digits than the English method, which only combines repeated digits (one eight two seven double-five six seven).

Association

Numbers become even more memorable if you can associate them with something that has meaning for you. Many people rely on personal associations to help them to commit numbers to memory. The following examples were given to me by people:

> *I remember the end of my fiance's phone number – 125 – because he likes trains. Once I've remembered the end, the beginning just attaches itself!*

Today I was given the number 7618 to remember as the security code to get into my building. I remember that because 76 is the number of trombones in the big parade, and 18 is the legal age for going to a pub.

I remember my padlock number 4832 because four eights are 32.

As a history teacher, I remember that the Magna Carta was signed in 1215 by imagining that it was done at lunchtime and that there was a clock in the background showing 12:15

These are examples of the mind being allowed to play to one of its strengths, that of making associations. However innumerate you might think yourself to be, there are almost certainly numbers that have special associations for you. The year you were born, the day of the month, your house number and so on. Looking for these familiar numbers buried away in a number you are trying to memorise can make it considerably easier to recall. Such tactics don't always help you to remember the whole number, but they can still help in getting part of it right.

Was that phone number 973 1966 or was it 973 1696? It was the first, because I remember thinking '1966', the year England won the World Cup.

Often you will have the opportunity to create an ID number or password yourself, and in these circumstances it makes perfect sense to use a number with which you have personal associations. The only disadvantage is that people tend to be predictable, for example by using their year of birth as a four-digit code. For your own security, you might want to play around with your familiar number; for example, by reversing the order of the digits, or by using an obvious pattern but adding a twist at the end (e.g. 1239 or 543218).

The more familiar you are with numbers and their properties, the easier it will be to find patterns in numbers that make them memorable. There is a story of a brilliant mathematician called Ramanujan who was ill in hospital. His friend, another mathematician called Hardy, came to visit him. Hardy said he had come by taxi, and that he had noted the taxi happened to have the number 1729.

'I'm sorry the number wasn't something more interesting,' said Hardy.

'Not at all, it is a most interesting number,' said Ramanujan. '1729 is the only number which is the sum of two cubic numbers in two different ways.'

It turns out that $1729 = (10 \times 10 \times 10) + (9 \times 9 \times 9)$, and is also equal to $(12 \times 12 \times 12) + (1 \times 1 \times 1)$. That fact might leave you cold, but to somebody like Ramanujan, it made the number both fascinating and extremely memorable.

Turning numbers into words

What if numbers carry no meaning for you? There is a technique that you might find extremely powerful. This does require some investment of time – a few minutes a day for several days – but once you have mastered it, you can apply the technique to any number that you need to commit to your memory.

The principle of the technique is to turn numbers that are unmemorable into words that are memorable. For example, the number 927 probably has no meaning for you and is therefore relatively unmemorable, but a word like 'Pink' immediately conjures up images and connotations that you can relate to, and this helps it to stick in the mind. (As will be revealed shortly, the memorable word 'Pink' represents the less memorable number 927 in this system.) The idea, then, is to have a system for converting numbers into words, so that you can memorise the word and then, when needed, you can convert that word back into the number it represents. If you think that by this time tomorrow you would probably have forgotten the number 927 but could still remember the word 'Pink' then you can see the benefit of the technique.

There are a number of competing systems that claim to be able to do this. To avoid confusion, I am going to describe only one such system, said to have been devised by Gregor von Feinaigle in the early 1800s. This system has survived the test of time, and is the most popular and practical.

In von Feinaigle's system (which is also referred to as Furst's System and the Major System), each digit is assigned a different consonant. To go any further, you have no choice but to remember what each letter stands for, but this is not too taxing:

1 is t (the letter t has one down stroke)
2 is n (the letter n has two down strokes)
3 is m (m has three down strokes – easy so far)
4 is r (r is the fourth letter of four)
5 is l (the Roman l stands for 50, which is close)
6 is j (a j is like a backwards 6)
7 is k (the letter k is a bit like two sevens stuck together at odd angles)
8 is f (because a cursive f looks a bit like an 8)
9 is p (because p is like a backwards 9)
0 is z (because z is for zero)

And that's it. Test yourself a few times, and these slightly odd associations will become familiar.

You now have the basics of being able to turn digits into words. Earlier, I gave the example of the number 927. Converted into consonants, this becomes P N K. To make a word, all you have to do is add vowels (which don't count as digits and can therefore be ignored when it comes to converting the word back into its number). In the case of P N K there are two obvious words, P i N K or P u N K, both of which are memorable. So if you had to remember the number 927 for a padlock, you might picture a Punk, or maybe the Pink

Panther, or even a Punk with Pink hair undoing the padlock. If the number ever escapes you, think of the associated word or image, and then convert that back into the number.

Although this method can be used to commit any number to memory, it is perhaps most useful as a check to make sure that you have got the order of digits right for a number you need to remember. In a couple of days' time, if you try to remember the number I quoted at the start of this section, you may have difficulty remembering whether it was 972 or 927. You will, I suspect, have less difficulty remembering whether it was PKN or PNK, since the association with Pink will come back to you, and hence so will the number.

It may have struck you that the system as I have described it only uses ten of the available twenty consonants. The method can be extended to use eighteen of the consonants, which gives you far more choice when it comes to creating memorable words or phrases. The extended version of the system is described in Appendix 2.

Although I said this system is well-suited to people who have no affinity with numbers, I can vouch for the fact that it can be just as useful to those with a more mathematical inclination. Many is the time that I have forgotten the order of the digits in my PIN number, and therefore had to say to myself the word 'Pomegranate' to bring it flooding back. (Except of course my keyword isn't pomegranate – I'm not *that* stupid.)

One final point. At a party, I once told a fellow

student that I had no difficulty remembering phone numbers, and that I could easily commit hers to memory. It is somewhat painful to think back to this rather feeble and transparent chat-up line, but to this day, twenty years later, I can remember that the number was 'Come show me no man', which translates back to 7363232. And would you believe it, whoever that girl was, I can't remember her name.

Orders of magnitude

Mount Everest is 29,035 feet high. British Telecom's annual turnover in 2002/3 was £20,812 million. Last year, 436 people in the USA were allegedly struck by lightning.

There is a vast mass of numerical facts relating to every topic you can think of. Often these numbers are quoted to five or even ten significant figures. To a few people, the precise details are important. After all, Sir Edmond Hillary would probably have missed out on a knighthood if he'd omitted the final 35 feet of his great climb. Quiz show contestants and physicists may also need to know numbers down to the last decimal place. However, for most of us, most of the time, it is not important to remember these numbers to the last digit. In fact I would go further and say that often the details of numbers get in the way of seeing the big picture.

However, it can be helpful to remember orders of magnitude. Knowing that Everest is exactly 29,035 feet high is of little general interest, but knowing that it is *approximately* 30,000 feet high (or about 9,000 metres) is helpful when being told that your aircraft is flying at 32,000 feet ('wow, if we were flying past Everest it would be almost at eye level', or more seriously, 'at this altitude we have no risk of flying into any land mass'). Similarly, when you hear that the record altitude for a manned balloon ascent is well over 100,000 feet, you can appreciate how phenomenally high that is.

If statistics can be linked to numbers that you are already familiar with, they will be easier to appreciate and also easier to remember. There are various rough statistics that I use as benchmarks when trying to picture the significance of other numbers I hear, for example:

- 10 metres per second is roughly the top speed of a sprinter (the world record for 100 metres being about ten seconds).
- 100,000 is about the seating capacity of an international sports stadium.
- 50 million is roughly the population of England.

Note that each one is a nice round number. You could add many more to this list. Each fact can form a useful link to a new number that you encounter, which in turn will help you to remember that number, or at least its order of magnitude.

So what about memorising statistics accurately, such as the number of yards in a mile (1760) or the year of the Battle of Agincourt (1415)? You can use the techniques described earlier in the chapter, or, if the statistic is sufficiently important to you, you may find that it just sticks. Knowing such statistics doesn't do any harm, but unless you have a special need, they belong firmly in the 'aspirational' and 'peripheral' zones of things to remember.

The Right Kind of Memory

Adam's job is to help companies that are in danger of going out of business. He told me that one of his biggest memory concerns was with numbers. 'Some of my colleagues have an amazing ability to quote numbers back to me, like the number of car sales in the UK or details of the annual staff growth for the last few years.'

Later in our conversation I asked him how profitable was the client he is currently working with?

'Oh, they made about £10 million last year.'

And how many people work there?

'It's about 400 or so across Europe.'

This ability to quote ballpark figures with such confidence showed he had no problem with numbers at all. In fact, it would have been rather disconcerting, maybe even a sign of obsession, if he had been able to quote £10.48 million profit or 386 staff off the top of his head.

12
How to Remember Facts

Topics covered

- Hints on studying
- Popular mnemonics
- Inventing mnemonics
- Tips for good mnemonics
- The power of Google

In past generations, learning facts was something that was associated with what you did at school. Once you had left school, you could relax. As George Savile, Marquis of Halifax, famously remarked more than 300 years ago: 'Education is what remains when we have forgotten all that we have been taught.'

Things have changed somewhat. There is now far less emphasis on learning facts than there used to be, so school pupils need to commit fewer facts to memory than previous generations. On the other hand, we live in an era of 'life-long learning', so even if you are not currently studying for exams, there is a chance that you might find yourself in this position at some time in the future. In many subjects, particularly the sciences, and professions like law, medicine and accountancy, fact-learning is still important, sometimes more so than in many school subjects.

You don't need be a student to want to learn facts, of course, and everything that follows is just as relevant to the layperson interested in acquiring knowledge as it is to somebody with a special need to memorise information.

Hints on studying

The amount of time that you spend learning is not nearly as important as the way that you learn. There are effective and ineffective ways of committing things to memory, and naturally it's the first type that we all seek.

Perhaps the most crucial factor in determining whether facts stick or not is your interest in the subject. This can often be observed in children (remember the example of James in the Introduction).

I met one ten-year-old who was unable to tell me any of the famous cities in continental Europe and his spelling of many common words was poor. Nevertheless, he could tell me in intricate detail the names, spellings and dates of every one of the vast number of dinosaurs described in his book on the subject. Why? Because he loved poring over the book, reading and rereading it with total fascination. He made no obvious effort to learn its contents; they simply stuck thanks to the total concentration and the enthusiastic repetition.

The novelty of subjects can make them more exciting for children, and they are better than adults at focusing exclusively on a subject without distraction, so long as it has grabbed their attention. So, as an adult, if you want to match the learning achievements of children, you may need to work harder or to 'work smarter' (maybe both).

Here are some tips:

The environment you learn in

Choose a quiet environment where you can concentrate. Children are often able to absorb information even when surrounded by distractions. Adults find this more difficult. If you are going to be taking an exam, try learning in a similar environment to the one in which you will be tested (remember the mascot-and-lavender principle in Chapter 9).

Time of day

Are you a morning person or an evening person? It helps to study when you are at your most alert, rather than when you are tired. Concentration briefly dips after a big meal as your body's resources are temporarily diverted towards digestion (the after-lunch syndrome), so it might pay to take a breather after you eat. However, don't allow yourself to get hungry as that will certainly detract from your ability to concentrate. There is some evidence that for the average person, learning in the evening and 'sleeping on it' can be marginally more effective than learning in the morning, but your personal preference should overrule this.

Work in short sessions

Research suggests that learning in short, spaced-out

sessions is better than cramming everything into one sitting. Four sessions of 30 minutes, spaced out by half hour gaps doing something completely different, are more effective than two solid hours.

Make it more organised and interesting

Chapter 8 explained the principles of how to make things more memorable. You should try to organise information into logical categories, and personalise it by linking it to things you already know. Make notes as you read – highlight the parts that are most interesting, put question marks next to the parts that you don't understand. One way to personalise information is to create mnemonics (see the next section).

Test yourself

Don't read through everything you have to learn in one go; stop regularly to test yourself, perhaps at the end of every page. Being tested seems to be out of fashion because doing badly can make you feel as if you have failed, but failing is the best way of knowing whether you have learned something or not. The very act of getting something wrong and being corrected is likely to make it more memorable. Don't be ashamed to fail a test.

Review

What really makes things stick is reviewing after taking a breather. Practice keeps your memories fresh, and also identifies the areas that are weak and need boosting. The increased time intervals between study described on page 161 can be an efficient way of making information stick.

As an overall strategy, these tips should considerably help you in your ability to store and remember facts. But remember, nothing beats a fascination for the subject you are trying to learn. If you find the subject dull, track down the books that are deemed the most accessible and fun. Go to a talk by somebody who is regarded as an inspirational teacher. Best of all, why not prepare a talk or a lesson on the subject for you to give to an audience? As any teacher will tell you, nothing helps you to learn facts better than having to teach them. If your audience is under ten years of age even better, because they won't let you get away with it unless you make the subject lively and accessible. (Older children or adults are more able to fake interest while quietly nodding off.)

Famous mnemonics

Although a 'mnemonic' is any kind of memory aid, it is normally applied to catchy little sayings that make some important but easily forgotten fact more memorable. ('Mnemonic' is an odd word, the only one in the English language that begins with 'mn', and all the more odd because its 'm' is silent. It comes from the name Mnemosyne, the Greek goddess of memory.)

Ask somebody to come up with a mnemonic they

remember and they are likely to come up with examples like these:

Richard of York Gave Battle in Vain – the initial letters of the colours of the rainbow; Red, Orange, Yellow, Green, Blue, Indigo, Violet.

Every Good Boy Deserves Football – or hundreds of variations on this theme – for the notes on the lines of the treble music stave.

I before E except after C – for knowing how to spell words like achieve and receive.

My Very Eager Mother Just Served Us Nine Pizzas – the order of the planets in the solar system, from Mercury to Pluto.

A Bactrian has two humps, like a B, and a Dromedary has one hump, like a D – for remembering the two types of camel.

You might be able to think of few more, though the set of widely known mnemonics is surprisingly small, twenty at most, and when lists of mnemonics are published they rapidly move from information that is of relevance to the general public to items that are so esoteric that they are only of interest to medical students and geologists.

A mnemonic isn't very helpful if, when recalling it,

you are prone to making an error and therefore coming up with the wrong 'fact'. This problem can even arise with some popular mnemonics, for example:

In fourteen hundred and ninety-two
Columbus sailed the ocean blue

This is a catchy little rhyme, but I listened to a group of people trying to recall it. Their conversation went something like this:

Steven: In sixteen hundred and seventy-two.

Audrey: No, I don't think it was that …

Steven: Well I remember it ended with seventy-two.

Janice: I think it was more like fifteen hundred.

Steven: That's it, in fifteen hundred and NINETY-two …

Audrey: Are you sure about that?

Remembering the Months

Thirty days hath September,
April, June and November,
February hath twenty-eight alone
All the rest have thirty-one

This is one of the most famously quoted of all mnemonics, and very useful too, so long as you can remember it. Unfortunately on the evidence of my research, the majority of people get no further than the first line, which makes this alternative version more appropriate:

Thirty Days hath September ... all the rest I can't remember

Inventing mnemonics

The famous mnemonics are fun, but the most useful mnemonics are the ones people invent for themselves. They are usually quirky and often they are not memorable to anybody but their inventor, but that's fine since their sole purpose is to help their user to remember things that matter to them. Personal mnemonics invented for some particular piece of trivia can be very valuable at times.

Melanie recently moved to Portland, Oregon, on the West Coast of the USA. Running through the city is the river Wilamet, a name that Melanie had difficulty pronouncing. Her inability to say the word properly marked her out as an incomer to the region. Somebody pointed out to her a nice local saying: 'It's Wil*ammit dammit.*' And she hasn't had a problem since!

Personal mnemonics can sound extremely convoluted to other people. For example, I came across somebody using the following spelling aid:

Eddie Died In November Buried Under Robert Green's House

…and the initials spell out the word 'Edinburgh'. Talk about a sledgehammer to crack a nut! In fact with mnemonics like these, sometimes it becomes necessary to know the fact in order to recreate the mnemonic that was supposed to help you in the first place. 'Let's see, it's something like Eddie died in Robert Green's House, no that can't be right, E D I N B … Eddie died in N B … what did N B stand for …?'

And so on. But I assume it worked for the person who invented it.

Tips for effective mnemonics

If you are making up your own mnemonics, there are a few tips for making them more memorable.

Concentrate on the important bits

Don't waste effort remembering the things that you are unlikely to forget anyway. Above I mentioned a convoluted mnemonic for spelling the word 'Edinburgh'. It used nine words to spell out the nine letters of the city. That was over the top. If you do happen to have problems spelling Edinburgh, it won't be the start of the word that you are going to misspell. It's the 'urgh' part that is likely to be hard to remember, the most common confusion being 'is it Burgh or Borough?' That's the part where a mnemonic would be more helpful.

Something like 'Urgh, it's Edinburgh' works. In the same vein, I quite like the mnemonic 'A fri*end* will always be there in the *end*'.

Use rhymes and rhythm

Rhymes and rhythm make something much easier to commit to memory, a trick that advertisers have exploited for decades. Think of some of the most famous slogans of old:

Beanz meanz Heinz

Murray Mints, too good to hurry mints

For mash get Smash

Often these slogans are more successful than the products they are advertising, living on in the memory long after the product has ceased to exist ('You do the Shake and Vac, and put the freshness back …').

As is clear from those examples, quality poetry is not required to make something memorable. In fact cheesy rhymes can be more memorable than slick ones. For example:

In 1666, London burned like sticks

Memorable Poems

I once split a class of children into two groups to try to commit a poem to memory. The first group I gave a poem by Ogden Nash called 'The Termite'. It begins:

Some primal termite tapped on wood,
and tasted it and found it good

(and continues in similar vein.)

To the other group I gave a poem called 'View of a Pig' by Ted Hughes, which begins

A pig lay on a barrow, dead
He weighed, they said, as much as three men ...

The language in the Nash poem is slightly more difficult, yet thanks to its rhymes and simple beat, the children committed it accurately to memory much more rapidly than they did the Hughes poem.

Use positive links, not negative ones

Sometimes people invent mnemonics that involve opposites. For example you might hear the comment: 'I remember how to turn this key because it's the opposite to the way that I would expect.' Mnemonics like this often go wrong, because after a while it becomes unclear what it is that needs to be revered. Jean described such a situation:

> *I bought a new car, and couldn't remember which side the petrol cap was on. I got it wrong a couple of times, so taught myself that the cap is on the opposite side to the side I'm used to. Unfortunately the next time I got it wrong again, because I'd got used to it being on the correct side!*

Jean replaced her negative mnemonic with a positive one: 'Right is right.' And she hasn't had a problem since.

Another example where a positive mnemonic would be helpful is the wiring of a plug. The bureaucrat who invented the colour scheme for the wires seems to have had no sense of the importance of making something memorable by easy association. The colours are:

Live – brown
Neutral – light blue
Earth – green and yellow stripes

These colours are completely counter-intuitive. It would have been far more natural to choose dangerous wasp stripes for the Live, brown for the Earth and something neutral like magnolia for Neutral. When trying to remember which colour goes where, some people use opposites, for example 'brown is *not* earth'. This is a classic case of a poor negative mnemonic, since the consequence of a mistake could be electrocution.

Humour and vulgarity

Funny things seem to be memorable, and naughty things seem to be even *more* memorable. Perhaps this is because when we hear them, we are inclined to pass them on to others, and this helps to fix the memory in the person doing the telling. Or maybe it's the heightened emotion associated with laughter when you hear the mnemonic that makes it stick. Medical students forced to digest tomes of facts are renowned for inventing coarse mnemonics to help them to remember. For example, the mnemonic for a particular set of veins is: *As She Lay Flat, Oscar's Passion Slowly Mounted*. And if you think that is slightly risqué, you should see the alternatives that were, alas, unfit to print in this book, though considerably more memorable. The ability of most doctors to regurgitate crude mnemonics of this kind (usually they grin as they do so) testifies to the power of this technique.

The power of Google

Not every fact that you are going to need has to be stored in your memory. In fact, every day you are bound to encounter situations where you don't have all the information at your fingertips. At these moments, the critical part of retrieving information comes not in knowing the facts but in knowing *how* to retrieve them.

Traditionally, this has been done in two ways. One is looking up the fact in a reference book, if you happen to have the appropriate one to hand. The other is by asking somebody who is likely to know the answer. A diverse set of friends with different interests can provide a valuable back-up for your own knowledge. (Have you ever wondered who would be your 'Phone a friend' choices if you were ever to be on the TV show *Who Wants to Be a Millionaire?*)

However, there is now another source of knowledge that is more powerful than either of the traditional methods of fact retrieval. The World Wide Web may be composed of 99 per cent junk, but the other 1 per cent still makes it the largest library of information in the world. As well as being a source of knowledge, the web can act as an extension to our ability to recall facts.

John described how he used the web to help him to recall the name of a well-known bookshop:

> *I couldn't recall the name, but I could think of other facts about it. The shop has a café, and I know there is at least one outlet in London. I also thought that it began with the letter 'B'. So I turned to my computer, and used the internet search engine google.com. I searched using the keywords* bookshop, London *and* café *and scanned the results. The third entry had the answer I was looking for, Borders.*

I should confess to using such an approach myself. I only half-remembered the quotation about education near the start of this chapter. I knew it was about education remaining when we've forgotten everything else, but couldn't remember the exact quote, nor who said it.

Google proved to be a powerful aid, though it required some trial and error to find the appropriate key words – *education, remains, everything, forgotten* – to unearth the full quotation. This also revealed one of the imperfections of the web as a memory tool. The quotation originally comes from George Savile, but on the Web it is widely attributed to Albert Einstein and to B.F. Skinner, both of whom were presumably quoting the original. It's as if the web in this case is mimicking the brain. Once an error is introduced, it gets reproduced until the new 'fact' has displaced the original one in the computer-network's memory. It is, I suppose, reassuring to know that even technology isn't perfect.

13
How to Remember Sequences, Stories and Jokes

Topics covered

- Using stories to remember lists
- The room method
- Remembering stories
- Remembering jokes

One of the most powerful ways of remembering is through stories. Humankind has used stories to pass on information since ancient times, and it is possible to tap into this natural aptitude of the brain to use stories to help you to remember lists or sequences. In this chapter I will discuss a couple of ways in which you can use stories or journeys to help you to remember. Story techniques tend to be very effective in the short term – a few hours or maybe a day or two.

However, details of stories will tend to fade after a while, and this raises a separate issue about stories and memory. While most people can remember the moral of a story and how they felt about it, sometimes the other information in a story can be frustratingly elusive. What was the plot? Who were the main characters? Occasionally you might want to actually remember a story in its own right, either as an anecdote, or maybe in the form of a joke. These aspects of stories are also discussed in this chapter.

Using stories to remember lists and sequences

Suppose you are confronted with having to remember a list of items. These might be your shopping list for today, or a sequence of things that occur to you on a 'to do' list while you are waiting at a bus stop. Here is just such a random list:

Gas bill
Stapler
Toy chicken*
Headphones
Pencil sharpener
Tennis racquet
Compact disc
Answerphone
Birthday card

If a list of unstructured thoughts crops up and you don't have a way of sorting them into useful categories, a quick and effective way of holding onto them is to link them in the form of a story. It doesn't matter if the story is feeble or implausible, as long as you make links between each element. The more graphic the story, the more likely its elements are to stick. For example,

Don't laugh, I really did have to remember to buy a toy chicken recently.

taking the above items in sequence you might create a story like this:

> *Bill the gas man had a cruel habit. He liked to staple together toy chickens, muffling the noise by wearing thick headphones. He would then sharpen their beaks using a pencil sharpener, before hitting them with a tennis racquet, aiming to get their beaks into the hole in the middle of a compact disc stuck on the wall. He would record all of this on his answerphone, which he would then post to his friend with a birthday card.*

One reading of that little story might be enough to make all of the items stick, certainly for as long as it takes you to find a piece of paper to write the items down.

This story method was often recommended for contestants trying to memorise items on the conveyer belt in the TV show *The Generation Game*. As each new item appeared before him (hair curlers, portable tape deck, cuddly toy) the contestant would add it on to his increasingly surreal story. It can take a couple of seconds to add an item onto a story, so it would take practice to make it work quickly enough to assimilate all the items.

The room method

There is a more structured, and for many people more powerful, technique for remembering lists and sequences called the room method. The room method has been popular since the time of the Ancient Greeks, and taps into the brain's natural aptitude for spatial and visual memory.

To use the room method, you need to have a clear picture in your head of a room, or a building, with which you are familiar, in which you mentally 'place' the items you want to remember. To retrieve the items, you then take a mental stroll through the building and pick up the items as you go.

For example, let's suppose the building you use is a regular house, with a front door leading onto a hallway, with a front room leading to a dining-room, then the kitchen, upstairs to a bathroom and then a bedroom.

Let's test out the room method using another list (don't worry about what this list is for!):

Dog
Umbrella
Toes
Nun
Scissors
Calculator
Elvis Presley
50 pence piece

Here is how you would use the room method to remember these items. I have deliberately made the images exaggerated, since that generally makes them more memorable:

At the front door, picture the door knocker as a dog, so when you thwack it, it goes 'Woof, woof, woof!' As you step inside, picture that your way is blocked by a pushed-up umbrella which you struggle to get past. Into the front lounge you see that each chair is the shape of a toe, attached to a central foot. In the dining room, at the table you discover a nun crossing herself before she starts to eat. You find that the kitchen has been snipped in half by a giant pair of scissors. Walking up the stairs, each step is a calculator button so you step on 1 + 1 + 1 + 1 =, with the answer displayed at the top step. From the bathroom you hear the sound of Elvis singing 'Love me Tender' as he takes a shower. And as you enter the bedroom you notice the mattress has seven sides and is silver coloured, resembling a 50 pence piece.

To make this work, don't just read the story, form a picture of each item as you progress through the house. Then shut the book and see if you can recreate your journey, collecting your eight items as you mentally walk through the house.

If you find visualisation easy, then you will probably find this technique surprisingly powerful. I have certainly witnessed just how effective it can be, with adults and with children. On one occasion as an experiment I gave a class of children a list of twenty items to remember in two minutes, like the old 'Kim's Game'. When I then tested them, their powers of recall varied enormously, from a lowest score of two to a high of thirteen, and with an average score of just under ten. I then got them to memorise a different list using the room method. The average score rose to about fifteen, but most dramatically, the boy who had scored only two using his unstructured memorisation of the first list improved his score to nineteen using the room method. Needless to say he was delighted.

Can you still remember the list of items I gave you just now using the room method? If you can, it's worth persevering with this simple system, and maybe expanding it. I gave you the layout of my own home, but the method works better if you adapt it to your own familiar surroundings.

You don't have to stick with one item per room. In fact, you should easily be able to use several features in each room. For example in your mind-kitchen you can put one item to remember on the fridge, another in the oven, and a third in the sink. If you want to remember things in a particular order, you need to have a fixed order in which you visit the various features of the room or building.

The Greeks seem to have used the room method mainly for memorising speeches – a task for which it is well suited, since the order in which you deliver items in a speech is important, and is easy to retain as long as the order in which you visit the rooms is clear. According to one source, the use of the room method for recalling speeches is the origin of the expression, 'In the first place, I did such-and-such'.

The need to memorise speeches in modern life is not so pressing. It is rare for you to need to give a talk without the benefit of notes or slides around which you can structure your thoughts. So the most likely application for the room method in your everyday life is to remember a sequence of things you need to do in the near future – a diary of activities for later today, for example – on those occasions where you haven't got a bit of paper to hand. It is also a good way of exercising your brain, as I explained on page 176. Or of course you might just want to amaze your friends with a party trick for remembering a list of items in any order they choose. That was a popular Victorian pastime, and it's always said that they knew how to make their own entertainment in those days …

Remembering stories

The story method and the room method use similar principles to help you to remember a group of unconnected items. Both methods might help you to remember a list for several days. However, after a while the details will usually begin to fade. In the same way, the details of 'real stories' often fade rapidly after we first encounter them.

It's common for people to get frustrated with their inability to remember the details of a story or its plot despite enjoying it at the time. Sometimes the details of a plot can vanish from recall within days. Jenny told me:

I recently went to see a special screening of North by Northwest *with my husband. I really enjoyed it, and when we met up with friends a couple of days later I was keen to tell them all about it. I was able to tell them it was a classic Hitchcock thriller, and that there were some great scenes like Cary Grant being attacked by a crop-spraying plane, and a scene at the end where they were clinging onto the carved faces on Mount Rushmore. However, I found it impossible to string the plot together. I found myself wondering, 'Why did all these things happen? What was the sequence of events?' I found it really difficult to recount the plot without getting it muddled, and finally I gave up.*

Many people (including me!) identify with Jenny's frustration. What is reassuring, though, is that while the details of the plot might be quickly forgotten, some things about a story will stick for a long time – in particular our feelings about it, and the lessons that we learned from it.

Margaret, a former neighbour of mine, is a good example of this. She is an avid book reader, and once she has read a book, she likes to keep it. The shelves in her lounge are packed with novels, biographies and histories that demonstrate her diverse tastes. On one occasion she showed me around her library. As we studied what was on the shelves, several times she admitted that she couldn't remember what a particular book was about it. Yet for every single book, even if she couldn't remember the contents, she had comments to make, such as 'This was one of his late novels, a bit dark,' or 'This one is very funny', and 'I was so moved by this book, I remember weeping afterwards'. Her situation is not untypical, in that the emotions associated with a book last longer than the ability to recall the characters and other details.

Why does this happen? It's probably a by-product of the way the brain works. The most important part of a story in the long term is the moral. A story can be wrapped up in lots of different ways (*Romeo and Juliet* became *West Side Story*, for example) but while the details differ, the overall message is the same.

But what if you do really *want* to remember the details of a story for more than a day or two?

The principles of how to make the plots and details of stories stick are the same as for every other type of memory.

Repetition is probably the most crucial element of all. Once you have read the story, write a summary of it (for yourself, or for somebody else). This repetition helps to make the story stick, and also identifies those parts that you have not fully registered. Once you have written a synopsis of your story, you could put this in the inside cover of the book. Rather than a straight summary, you could instead write a book review, saying what you liked or didn't like. The act of writing this review is important for your memory in the long term, and will be a great help even if you never read the review again.

To reinforce it, you could join a book club. Book clubs have become an extremely popular social activity, and the opportunity to talk about a book that you have read will also help to fix it in your memory in the long term.

You could write a review before you go to a meeting. This might be just for your own benefit to help you decide what you actually thought of the book. If you feel that you can convey your thoughts more clearly in writing than in talking, you could even read out your review at the book club meeting (though you should keep the review to just a few paragraphs or you might not be asked back).

Remembering jokes

One special category of story is jokes. Most people enjoy jokes, but the majority also say that they have difficulty remembering them. Similar numbers of women and men report having difficulty remembering jokes, but it is normally only men who express this as something they wished they could improve. Although there are many female comedians, joke-telling remains a predominantly male thing. Jokes seem to serve an important part in male bonding, much more so than with women.

If remembering jokes is a more common concern than remembering stories, does this mean that jokes are harder to remember? Or is it just that it is more important to get a joke right? There are several theories.

First there is the 'twist' theory. What makes a joke funny is almost always the surprise twist at the end. In other words, a joke is not logical, or at least, it doesn't follow the path that our brain expects, which is why we find the punchline funny. This makes it very different from a romantic story, for example, where the finale is often only too predictable.

Take for example this joke, which psychologist Richard Wiseman reported as being the funniest in the world after conducting research across several countries:

> *Two hunters are out in the woods when one of them collapses. He doesn't seem to be breathing and his eyes are glazed.*
>
> *The other guy takes out his phone and calls the emergency services. He gasps: 'My friend is dead! What can I do?'*
>
> *The operator says: 'Calm down, I can help. First, let's make sure he's dead.' There is a silence, then a gunshot is heard.*
>
> *Back on the phone, the guy says: 'OK, now what?'*

As you read that joke, you could probably feel your brain anticipating where this story was going, and then being surprised when it went somewhere completely different, perhaps enough to create a laugh. Maybe it is this unexpected final leap in the joke that makes it hard to recall, because it doesn't go along a well-trodden logical path in the brain.

Alternatively, there is the repetition theory. Some people have a reputation as being good at telling jokes. You probably know such a person yourself. How do they achieve this enviable status? Almost certainly good joke-tellers enjoy the experience, and make a habit of telling jokes as often as they can. Nothing beats regular repetition for making it easy to remember something. By definition, therefore, good joke-tellers become good at remembering jokes. It becomes a virtuous circle of telling jokes, getting a laugh, wanting to repeat the experience, so telling the same jokes to the next group of people ... and so on. Therefore their repertoire of jokes remains wide, and their regular rehearsal ensures that the stories come out fluently.

Finally there is the anxiety theory. A joke only works if it generates a laugh at the end. A small mistake in the order in which you deliver the story, or in the wording of the punchline, makes all the difference between a joke being funny or falling completely flat. Unlike telling a story about your holiday, or recalling what happened to your favourite football team over the weekend, the stakes in telling a joke are extremely high, because if a joke doesn't generate a laugh then the teller has failed and everyone is embarrassed. This potential for messing up a joke can cause extreme anxiety – and of course anxiety is itself a major stumbling block to memory, which makes the joke even more likely to fail.

Most of us have had the unpleasant experience of telling an unfunny joke. So when asked if we can remember any jokes, what do we do? Do we attempt to spontaneously recreate without rehearsal the one we heard a couple of weeks ago about the nun on the golf course? Not likely! Instead, we lie to the audience, and perhaps to ourselves too, and say, 'No, I can't remember any.'

If you happen to be somebody who does, for whatever reason, want to remember more jokes, here are some suggestions:

- Choose jokes that follow a familiar pattern. (For example: 'A man walks into a bar …', or 'There are three people in a field, a banker, an engineer and a lawyer …', or even 'Knock, knock …') Jokes with familiar structures are easier to remember.
- Repeat jokes that you like as soon as possible after you hear them. Rehearse them to yourself (out loud) before you tell them.
- Keep a record of your favourites.
- Until you are confident in your joke-telling, choose small, safe audiences to try them out on.

14
How to Remember the Future

Topics covered

- Retaining things in the short term
- Routine
- Remembering a long-term action

Remembering the future sounds like a contradiction in terms, until you realise that you use your memory for the future all the time. You need to remember to switch off the lights when you leave the house later, to send a birthday card to your brother next week, to buy tickets for your holiday and so on.

'The future' can be anything from a year or more to just a few seconds, and the two ends of the time spectrum present different challenges when it comes to forgetting.

Call Me Unreliable

People's strengths for different types of memory will vary, and it's partly down to luck as to how strong you are in each type. However, the way we view people with poor memories depends a lot on where their weakness happens to be.

What they forget	How we describe them
Forgetting past events:	They 'have a bad memory'
Forgetting where things are put:	They are 'forgetful'
Forgetting names:	They seem 'rude/not interested in others'
Forgetting appointments:	They are 'unreliable'

Retaining things in the short term

Here is a situation that might sound familiar. You are in deep conversation with somebody about something that you are planning together. As your colleague responds to your last comment, it occurs to you that there is something else that you meant to tell him. When he finishes talking, you say, 'And there was another thing … Oh, what was it?' In those few moments between thinking of what you wanted to say and having a chance to say it, the thought has leaped from your grasp like a trout squirting from your hands back into a stream.

Or maybe you are driving down the motorway, hands on the wheel, daydreaming a bit, when several ideas occur to you for things that you need to do over the weekend. Yet when you are finally able to free your hands and find a pen and paper, those ideas have maddeningly disappeared.

This is a common experience for many people. The problem of a thought disappearing before you have had a chance to record it arises when, for whatever reason, you fail to transfer something from your short-term or working memory into your longer-term memory. Since the capacity of our working memory tends to diminish as we age, the problem is more common among the elderly than the young, though even teenagers are likely to experience it at times.

There are several ways to overcome this problem, drawing on principles and techniques described elsewhere in this book. For example, you might consider the following:

Carry a notebook and pen

This is the most basic but practical suggestion. When those little thoughts occur, as you are strolling on a walk or lying in bed unable to sleep, a notebook and pen can be invaluable. You can even use a notebook mid-conversation, though it might appear a little eccentric. Maybe you should keep one notebook in your wallet, and another on your bedside table. Between the two of them, this should cover you for most eventualities.

Go back through the conversation for a cue

This tactic comes naturally to most people. If you have lost a train of thought or an idea, recap what you were talking about earlier. More often than not, some part of that conversation was responsible for triggering your idea and will do so again when you revisit it.

Say it aloud or form an image

If a thought comes to you that you need to hold onto, you can help to etch it more permanently if you either say it out loud (assuming this is suitable in the circumstances) or form an image in your mind. So, for example, if you are driving and the sudden thought is 'Must buy dog food on the way home', look at some feature of the car, such as the glove compartment, and imagine opening it and a dog barking as a tin of Doggo rolls out. You still need to remember that you've got something to remember, but at least when you look at the glove compartment, you should have little difficulty making the link.

Use the story or room method

The story and room methods described in Chapter 13 are both useful short-term memory aids if you have more than one item to remember, particularly if the sequence is important.

The best advice of all is to act on a thought as soon as you are able to. It can sometimes take only a few seconds for you to be distracted from something that you intend to do – as the story in the box 'Age-activated Attention Deficit Disorder' makes plain.

Age-activated Attention Deficit Disorder (AAADD)

Versions of the following story have appeared widely on the Web. As far as I know, the 'disorder' was just the invention of its now anonymous author, but the whole thing rings very true:

It's a nice day so I decide to clean the car; I start toward the door and notice there is some mail on the hall table. OK, I'm going to clean the car, but first I'll just go through the mail. I lay the car keys down on the table, throw away the junk mail and I notice the bin is full. OK, I'll just put the bills on the table and take the rubbish out, but since I'm going to be near the mailbox anyway, I'll pay these few bills first. Now, where is my new cheque book? I find it, and notice there's only one cheque left. My new cheques are in my desk, so I go to the study and on it is the half-finished bottle of juice I was drinking. I'm going to look for those cheques. But the juice is warm, so I decide to pop it into the fridge to chill it. I head towards the kitchen when I spot that the flowers in the vase need some water. I set the juice on the counter and aha! – there are my glasses. I was looking for them all morning! I'd better put them away first. I fill the container with water and head for the flower pots — what! Someone left the TV remote in the kitchen! We will never think to look in the kitchen tonight when we want to watch TV so I'd better put it back in the lounge where it belongs. But first I must water the flowers. I splash some water onto the floor and put down the remote so I can wipe it up, then I head back down the hall trying to figure out what it was I was going to do.

End of day: the car isn't washed, the bills are unpaid, the juice is sitting on the kitchen counter, the flowers are half-watered, the cheque book still only has one cheque in it and I can't seem to find my car keys! When I try to figure out how come nothing got done today, I'm baffled because I know I was busy. I realise this is a serious condition and I'll get help. But first, I think I'll check my email.

Routine activities

Many things that you need to remember are things that you will need to do more than once. For example, you may need to take antibiotics every morning, or feed the neighbour's cat while they are away. If these are things that you are afraid you might forget, one of the best ways to remember them is to link them to some aspect of your daily routine that you never forget. So you might link taking your tablets to boiling the kettle for your morning tea. By leaving the tablets next to the kettle, you will automatically get a reminder. If you put the cat bowl outside the front door, you are reminded of it when you leave the house.

One clever device that Emily used to remind her to do a particular therapeutic exercise three times a day was to buy a roll of red stick-on tabs, and to stick them around the house at points where she was likely to go frequently. So at her house you will see a red dot on the door to the main rooms, on the teapot handle, on the fridge door, by the toothbrushes, on the TV remote and on dial of the iron. As she points out, she still has to remember what the red dot means, but that is not a problem for her. She just needs a prompt to remind her to do the exercises that she might otherwise forget.

Techniques like the red-dot method can be very effective, though their effectiveness can diminish with time as the person using them becomes accustomed to seeing them. After a while, seeing a red dot on a household object no longer provokes the reaction, 'What's that doing there?' and gradually it becomes invisible. If the effectiveness of the prompt is diminishing, come up with a new prompt – a different colour, or a different device altogether.

Remembering a long-term action

Just as often, the thing that you want to remember to do in the future is a one-off. These can be the most frustrating. For example, you might need to make an important phone call later today. During the day, you remember several times that you need to make this call, but when you remember, it is never at a convenient time. Then, when the moment comes when you could make the call, you are preoccupied with something else and forget.

How can you ensure that you are persistently reminded to do something until you have actually done it. Here are some ideas that different people suggested:

- Put a radio alarm by your desk, and when it goes off, press the 'Snooze' button so that the radio will come back on again in 10 minutes. This is a less irritating approach than setting an alarm to go off on your watch or phone, though that will also do the trick.
- If you spend much of your day at a computer and are a compulsive email-checker, send an email to yourself saying that you need to do the task later today. Leave the email unopened until the task is completed.
- Create a to-do list, and place it prominently in front of you. Tick off tasks when they are done.
- Tie a piece of string to something you expect to use at the time when you need to do the task. So, if the task could be done around the time when you have coffee, tie string to the handle of your mug.
- Delegate the task to somebody whom you can trust to do it.

All of these are physical aids, the equivalent of the infamous knotted hankie, and the evidence is that most people find these more reliable than mental aids.

There is, of course, one physical aid that I haven't mentioned yet in this chapter, which is more popular than anything else. That is the diary, the most ubiquitous memory tool of all. Diaries are usually closed books that sit on a desk, but around the house, the wall calendar is its equivalent. In fact the best memory-jogger of all is probably a wall diary that hangs somewhere prominent, with a pencil attached to it by string, and the main telephone next to it. With that combination, even the most disorganised person could hope to keep those missed appointments to a minimum.

15
How to Remember the Past

Topics covered

- Plan for the future
- Using technology
- Keep a diary
- Photo albums
- Alternative records
- Retrieve and rebuild the past

Plan for the future

The American columnist Herb Caen once said: 'I tend to live in the past because most of my life is there.' He was speaking for most people who are getting on in life. As people become less active, memory plays a growing part in their conversation, and reliving past experiences becomes an increasingly important source of pleasure.

How frustrating, then, if one's memories of the past begin to fade. It is as if part of your person is being taken away from you. Pensioners that I spoke to reported how whole episodes of their lives seemed to have disappeared – details of their first jobs, or perhaps important incidents in their family's history.

As I explained in Chapter 3, forgetting is inevitable, and the longer ago that memories were last retrieved, the more likely it is that the links to them will disappear, leaving them permanently lost.

Of all the things that we 'need' to remember, it is ultimately one's past that is the most important. Not that this is an issue when you are in your twenties, and your past is readily accessible while you energetically live for the present. But what you do in your twenties could be of enormous interest to you when you are in your seventies, both for your personal reflections and for the stories you want to tell others. Where did I live? How did I spend my working day? What were my opinions? Maybe this is easy to remember now, but will it be when you come to telling your grandchildren or great-grandchildren your life story?

I would argue that in the same way that a prudent person starts planning for their retirement, it is also a wise investment to plan now for your future memories. If you rely on your elderly brain to recall your life story for you, then you might be seriously disappointed.

Of all the things that you want to be able to remember, it is remembering the past where your brain needs the most help from external aids. And as with pensions, it's never too late to start preparing.

Often it is when life is in its most exciting phase that people have the least time or inclination to preserve the moments for posterity. (Do those folk who spend their entire holiday video-recording their experience ever actually enjoy the moment, or are they doing it entirely so that they can discover what they did on their holiday when sitting back on their home sofa?) So how can one most effectively preserve memories of today for the future?

Using technology

Walk into any grandparent's lounge and you'll see photos decking every horizontal surface. Almost always, they are family photos, particularly of the children and grandchildren at various stages in their lives. All of this is a reminder that photographs are the mainstay of our memory of the past.

There are of course many other ways to remember the past. Today the technology is available to build a very creative record of your life today, which will provide hours of nostalgic pleasure in years to come. However, the rapid advances in the ability to store information electronically also create a possible threat to preserving your memories in the long term.

Think of your computer documents from fifteen or twenty years ago, written using a program such as Word Star and stored on a five-inch floppy disk. The floppy disk was a wonderful advance when it came to storing information quickly and reliably, but where would you go now to find a computer that can read a five-inch floppy disk? And where would you find that old version of Word Star that would be able to read the file? Technology is changing at such a rate that today's recording medium may well be redundant in ten years' time. How annoying it would be to put together a complete audio-visual family history, only to discover that it couldn't be retrieved in thirty years' time without forking out a fortune to a special data-reading specialist!

So, if you do want to use technology to support your life memory, make sure that you transfer your records onto the latest devices, once they are established.

Oddly, therefore, when it comes to building your collection of memories, the oldest and simplest technologies may prove to be the best in the long term: pen on paper, printed photographs, and even perhaps long-playing records. (The technology for old-style 33 rpm records is sufficiently simple that it wouldn't take much investment for a company to start manufacturing the players again. This cannot be said of CD players, should that technology become redundant.)

The Past Won't Be Black and White

When today's retired community were young, they were recorded in black and white, smartly turned out with combed hair, with men wearing ties and women dresses. This all reinforces the impression that they belonged to a generation with fundamentally different values and beliefs. But it won't be long before retired people become fully available in Technicolor. If they were born in the 1960s, then the chances are that their entire lives will be represented by colour photographs, with them wearing casual dress and a range of mildly rebellious hairstyles. Quite what this will do to the way the young view the old, or the elderly view themselves, is uncertain, but it will certainly take some of the mystique out of aging, and it will bring the past that much closer. Following the colour generation will be the video generation, where grannies will not only been seen running around in their youth, but they will be audible with it. So much for that clichéd image of your parents having been seen but not heard.

Keep a diary

Diaries and journals have been the main form of memory preservation for centuries. Before embarking on diary-keeping, however, you might ask yourself who and what the diary is for. Is it for others to read when you are gone? Is it simply there as evidence in your defence when the finger gets pointed at you? Those certainly seem the main two reasons why many famous diarists kept their journals. It is a chance to tell the story accurately, at least from your point of view. But diaries don't have to be for other people. The most important audience for your diary is probably you – the you in ten, twenty or thirty years' time. This takes off some of the pressure, since you will forgive yourself for not writing in flowery, well-punctuated prose.

Think about what that 'you' will be wanting to read about. 'Went to the dentist' may be of some interest, but perhaps you will be more interested to know what the dentist was like, what she found when she was poking around, what music was playing in the background and what old magazines were lying around in the reception area.

People are often reluctant to start diaries because they don't think they will keep them up. On top of that, the prospect of putting in a full, daily record can become more like a chore that resembles homework.

It's important to dispel these myths. I came across several people who had kept diaries in the past, and none of them were anything like the meticulous daily records of, say, the politician Tony Benn. Here are two examples:

> *Most days were left blank, but those odd days where I did write down my thoughts make interesting reading – though the occasional single word or name no longer means anything to me!*

> *I spent a summer working in Paris, and kept a journal just for that short period. It was fascinating to remind myself of the thoughts and experiences of the time.*

Rather than recording your entire diary, why not have a journal in your desk in which you write up those particularly eventful days, like the time when your work project comes to fruition, or the day your first child or grandchild arrives. These exciting days are often so busy that there is little thought of writing them up, but they can be the most rewarding to relive later.

Photo albums

The great advantage of a photo album over a stack of photos is that it reduces the risk of shuffling the record out of order. Boxes of unfiled photos kept under the bed can make for an intriguing detective game later in life, but you can save a lot of effort if you sort them while the memories are still relatively fresh. Even a photo album can miss out on a lot of key information. 'Who is that woman standing next to Auntie Doris at our wedding?' I heard somebody ask. Annotating an album with captions may seem like overkill at the time, but ten years later you might well be grateful that you have recorded who is in the photo and where it was taken.

Most photos tend to be staged snaps of family and friends posing for the camera, but there is far more to your life than this. Why not spend an afternoon photographing some of your familiar local haunts – shops, shopkeepers, your local bus, the cars in the car park, the trees in the park? These are all things that are familiar to the point of ignoring them today, yet in 40 years they will probably all have disappeared or changed.

Why not switch to taking black-and-white photos of the family for a while? When everything is in colour, black-and-white photos can be more evocative and will also stand out from the crowd. Many photographers find black-and-white pictures are better at capturing mood than colour.

And albums don't have to be just photos. Printed materials can also evoke powerful memories later. Why not include in your albums some non-photographic material such as the menu of your meal that day, or the bus ticket, or the newspaper write-up of the play that you saw the evening before?

The main snag of photo albums is that they take up space, and if you hold onto everything (just in case it proves to be of interest later on) you'll be out of shelves in no time. Perhaps it's best to indulge in an occasional album cull, where you pick out the 10 per cent of the material that brings back the most memories, and dispose of the rest. You can save space, of course, by putting the less important photographs together into a collage and taking a colour photocopy of them. At least half the space on most photos is of unwanted background, so why not be ruthless and snip off the background trees?

Alternative records

Diaries and albums are the standard ways to store information from the past, but there are other, more creative ways of building your future nostalgia store. For example:

- Smells are the most evocative source of past memories. What smells of today can you save for tomorrow? Fabric from a piece of material, perhaps? A favourite perfume or aftershave? (Though be careful; smells will fade and change over time, especially if exposed to air.)

- Keep a record of your TV viewing over a whole week. What programmes did you watch, and what did you think of them? What did you think of the stars who appeared? Who's in and who's out? Record what you imagine TV will be like in twenty years' time.
- Keep a copy of a daily newspaper, or maybe a magazine that you read this week. Mark on it the stories that are of particular interest, and why. Sometimes it is things that are particularly on your mind today that will be most interesting to look back on when you are older.
- Wait until the tape on your answerphone is full, then remove it for safekeeping. A full tape of messages can provide a fascinating snapshot of your social life. There is a freshness and immediacy about a message left on an answering machine that a holiday photo or staged recording cannot capture.

Those are just suggestions, of course, and you probably don't want to turn your home into an instant museum. There has to be a balance between recording life and living it. On the other hand, you don't want to be kicking yourself when, aged 82, you have no records to jog your memory. It's all too easy to be so wrapped up in the day-to-day needs of a job or a family that you never allow yourself to step back and see the bigger picture. As John Lennon said in one of his songs: 'Life is what happens to you while you're busy making other plans.'

Retrieving and rebuilding the past

Depending on what stage of life you are at, you may now be looking backwards more than you are looking forwards. In which case, while you can still start to keep a diary and to put together albums, what's of more interest to you is retrieving your past while you are still well placed to do so. That's easy enough if you have kept all your past records, but considerably more difficult if you never got round to it.

One process that can be effective in bringing back memories is known as 'contextual reinstatement'. In everyday language this means going back to the scene and retracing your steps. If going back to the place where the memories were first formed is not possible, closing your eyes and imagining yourself back at the scene can sometimes work just as well.

Because all sorts of cues can help to retrieve memories, exploring specific areas that don't appear to relate to the thing you are trying to remember can also bring back fresh memories. For example, when trying to recall details of a journey that you made last month, on a Wednesday, try asking yourself the following questions:

- What did you eat that day? What would your lunch arrangements have been?
- What was on TV that day, that you might have wanted to watch?
- What were the news stories that day?
- Is there anything in particular that you or somebody close to you normally does on Wednesdays? What

happened with that regular activity on the Wednesday in question?

- What was the weather like that day?

You can probably think of other questions relating to seemingly peripheral details of the day. Each one has the potential to trigger relevant memories about your journey.

These principles also apply to bringing back memories from your more distant past. There are so many ways to think about your life story: where you lived, your jobs, your holidays, your musical tastes, your medical history. Each sequence will bring back its own memories, and these can be brought together to help you to compile the jigsaw.

Autobiographies Aren't Just for Celebrities

Have you ever thought of writing your autobiography? Your story may not have been sensational enough to merit being piled high in the window of Waterstones, but it will be a fascinating read for your family. It's a chance for you to convey who you are and were, and why you did the things that you did. Writing an autobiography would also make a challenging project in its own right. They say everyone has a book in them, and your autobiography could be yours. Nobody else can write it!

Final Thoughts: Coming to Terms with Memory Loss

You should now have a better understanding of how your memory works, and of some of the strategies and techniques that will help you to remember those things that you regard as important.

Three basic principles have returned time and again.

- You can make your life a lot simpler by *organising* those things you need to remember.
- The brain works by *association*, using information from all of the *senses*, and you can make things more memorable by exploiting the power of images, smells and sounds.
- *Repetition*, and testing your ability to *recall*, are the best aids to keeping your memory fresh.

By applying these principles, along with the other tips that appeal to you, you should notice an improvement in your ability to remember. However, nothing is fool-proof. Despite following all of these principles to the letter, you might still find yourself occasionally being frustrated by lapses in your memory. What should you do about this?

First, you should take comfort from the fact that you are not alone. There are millions of other people in the same situation. In fact there comes an age when the popular conversation at dinner parties is no longer comparing property prices or local schools but, instead, who can boast the most spectacular 'senior moment'. If you are at that age, at least you are now armed with plenty of anecdotal examples and techniques to show off to your peers. (If you can remember them, that is!)

If you are concerned that your ability to remember has severely declined, you should try to establish this more formally. Test your ability to remember items in a list over a period of a few weeks or months, and check your scores. Keep a record of your memory lapses, and see if you spot any patterns. Ask those who know you if they notice any changes. When doing this you should also concentrate on the positive aspects by keeping notes of those things that you successfully *remember*. This will help to put things in perspective.

If you believe that there are real signs for concern, the best person to consult is your GP. They will be in the best position to give you a detached, objective opinion, by asking you a few questions about your experiences with your memory and your lifestyle. Often after a short discussion, your GP will be able to reassure you that the lapses you are suffering are either perfectly normal, or are due to particular factors in your life at present, such as stress or lack of sleep. However, your GP might refer you to a memory clinic, where you can be assessed more thoroughly with some formal memory tests. If you have physical symptoms, or a history of head injury, you might be given a benign scan (an MRI scan is most common, though PET scans are slowly being introduced). These scans will show up any obvious anomalies in the brain that might be the cause of memory problems.

The most likely 'treatment' that will be recommended to you will be to give yourself some mental exercise. You might even be advised to read a book about memory. (If you are advised to read *this* book, you will have to produce your copy and tell your doctor that you've been there and done that!)

It is possible that you might be prescribed drugs. As discussed in Chapter 6, most prescribed drugs and alternative medicines have only a modest effect on memory in the long term, though they can in many cases significantly slow down deterioration. But things are changing all the time, and given the amount of investment into memory drugs, it would be disappointing if dramatic advances aren't made in the treatment of severe memory ailments in the next ten years.

In the meantime, think of some of the advantages of having a poor memory. If you've forgotten the stories of your friends, this means that you won't object to them telling you them again ... and again ... and again. And if your own stories of your past life are inaccurate, who cares, so long as they are entertaining? (In contrast, few things can be more annoying than being with somebody whose memory is so good that they can correct every last detail of what you have to say.)

And it's worth noting that there are worse things in life than having a bad memory. In the words of Albert

Schweitzer, 'Happiness is nothing more than good health and a bad memory.'

But I'll leave the last word to Agnes. I met her when I was visiting an elderly group, to ask them about memory problems and their tactics for overcoming them. Her response has stuck with me ever since:

Actually, all this talk about forgetting being bad and needing to remember is quite wrong. For me at my age, it's a perfect excuse for just about everything.

Appendix I

Memory self-assessment questionnaire

Tables A1 and A2 contain a simple questionnaire to allow you to get a rough assessment of your memory. It is adapted from questionnaires published by Alan Baddeley and others. To complete it, use the following scoring system.

Once a year or less 6
Two or three times a year 5
Once a month 4
Two or three times a month 3
Two or three times a week..2
Every day..1
Two or more times a day 0

I have put typical scores in the right-hand column, though I should point out that individuals who have completed the table often varied widely from these. When you have finished, add up all the points to give yourself an overall score.

Table A1: How often do you typically ...

	Your score	Typical score
Refer to a diary or calendar to remind you of what you need to do?		1
Use notes, reminders or other physical prompts to remind you to do things?		2

Table A2: How often would you say that you …

Find a word is on the 'tip of your tongue'?		3
Repeat to somebody something you told them or asked them earlier the same day?		5
Forget, or need to look up, a phone or other number that you use frequently?		3
Forget to do a task on the day that you said you would do?		5
Don't recognise a close friend or relative?		6
Forget the start of a magazine article and have to reread it?		4
Forget birthdays of people close to you?		5
Walk into a room and wonder what you are there for?		4
Don't recognise a place that you have been to many times?		6
Temporarily forget the names of family members or *close* friends?		5
Temporarily forget the names of other people that you know?		3
Can't recall what you did yesterday without serious effort or prompting?		4
Forget where things are normally kept in the house?		5

Add up your total score for A1 and A2. More than 70 points is high and an indication that your general memory serves you very well. A score of between 60 and 65 is much more typical. However, if you have a busy and varied schedule, or a lifestyle where you meet different people every day, you have far more opportunities to experience memory lapses, so your score might be lower.

A low score might also mean that you are not strong when it comes to organising your affairs. By making more use of a diary and other prompts, and by organising your home or your desk in a more logical way, your score should increase.

If you are concerned about a low score, ask somebody who knows you well to assess you using the same questionnaire. It might be that you are being too hard on yourself. If they come up with similar results, then that is a good indication that you might want to take active steps to improve your memory.

Appendix 2

Extension to the number-word system

In the simple form that I described the number-letter system in Chapter 11, each of the ten digits was assigned to one consonant. However, there is a limit to how many words you can make using just those letters. To give the method more flexibility, most of the remaining consonants can be allocated to the ten digits simply based on their sounds.

For example, number one is 't'. The mouth position used for 't' is very similar to that for 'd' and 'th', and in the extended system, they can therefore be used as alternatives for the number one. 'J' (six), 'sh' and 'ch' are almost identical sounds, so they become alternatives for six.

Using the similarity of sounds, the complete set of letters for digits in this system is as follows:

1 is t, th or d
2 is n
3 is m
4 is r
5 is l
6 is j, ch, sh or zh
7 is k, q, c (the hard 'c' as in 'count')
   or g (the hard 'g' as in 'goat')

8 is f, ph or v
9 is p or b
0 is z, s

All the vowels, plus the Y, W and H sounds, are ignored, so that the word Yellow actually represents the number 5 – the only relevant sound being a single 'l'. Notice how it is the sound of the word rather than the literal spelling that I use here, so 'll' in yellow is 5, not 55. That may seem confusing, but in fact it makes the method simpler to use, not least because it means you don't need to be able to spell accurately.

The letter 'x', which sounds like 'ks', represents the two digits 70. 'Cellophane' sounds like 'Selofane', so it represents the number 0582.

If you are converting a number into a memorable word, you will usually have plenty of choices. For example, the number 60957 can be represented in many different ways, such as 'Jezebel K', or 'Cheese block', or 'Jazz polka'. Choose whichever phrase you find the most memorable.

You might like to have a go at a few examples yourself. What word or words can you come up with to represent:

621

34092

847131

621 is JNT, so 'joint' or 'Janet' ; 34092 is MRZPN – 'marzipan' would fit; and 847131 is FRKTMT, so how about 'Freak Tomato'?

And what numbers are represented by the words:

Titanic

Bugs Bunny

Chocolate cake

Titanic – 1127; Bugs Bunny – 97092; Chocolate cake – 675177:

If you had to remember the numbers 1127, 97092 and 675177, or the words Titanic, Bugs Bunny and chocolate cake, which would you go for? I would certainly opt for the latter.

Match Wits With The Kids

A Little Learning for all the Family

Jonathan Green

'This jolly compendium will enlighten all who dip in … Green eserves 10/10.' – *Independent*

So, who was the first Tudor king?

What is a preposition, or a conjunction for that matter?

How exactly does photosynthesis work?

And what on Earth is 5^{-3} trying to tell us?

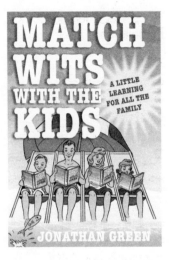

Experienced teacher and author Jonathan Green's detailed, witty lessons on English, maths, the sciences, history, geography, language and Classics will refresh your memory and answer the questions you were afraid to admit you needed to ask.

Just what you need to stay one step ahead of smart-alec children (or catch up with know-it-all grown-ups).

Paperback   UK £8.99   Canada $18.00
ISBN: 978-184831000-1

www.matchwits.co.uk

How to Remember (Almost) Everything Ever

Rob Eastaway

The perfect memory book for children.

Crammed with cool tricks, experiments, and great mind games.

Discover how to make and break secret spy codes.

Read about the amazing Russian man who could remember absolutely everything – ever!

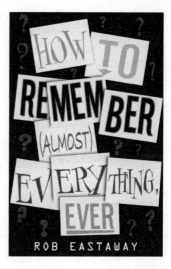

Impress your friends, amaze your teachers … and outsmart your parents.

Paperback   UK £5.99 Canada $12.00
ISBN: 978-1840467-97-0

Making Time

Why Time Seems to Pass at Different Speeds and How to Control it

Steve Taylor

'Provocative and freewheeling, wilfully unscientific without ever dabbling in pseudoscience, this book will really start you thinking about how you can try to be free.' – *Independent*

'A fascinating inquiry … Taylor's book is so absorbing that time will fly by as you read it.' – *Herald*

'A large part of this book's appeal is its willingness to engage in truly mind-bending theories … There is plenty to entertain us.' – *Nicholas Lezard, Guardian Paperback Choice of the Week*

'It is possible to alter our perceptions in order to make time pass quickly or slowly, just as we wish, and Taylor shows how it can be done.' – *Good Book Guide*

'A remarkable study of the mystery of time' – *Colin Wilson*

Why does time speed up as we get older? Why does time fly when we're having fun, or drag when we're bored? How can we learn to live in the present?

Paperback   UK £8.99
ISBN: 978-1848310-01-8

A Mind of Its Own

How Your Brain Distorts and Deceives

Cordelia Fine

'This is one of the most interesting and amusing accounts of how we think – I think.' – *Alexander McCall Smith*

'Witty and informative' – *Philip Pullman*

'A fascinating, funny, disconcerting and lucid book. By the end you'll realise that your brain can (and does) run rings around you.' – *Helen Dunmore*

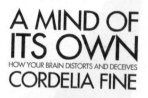

'Fine sets out to demonstrate that the human brain is vainglorious and stubborn. She succeeds brilliantly.' **Mail on Sunday**

'Fine slaps an Asbo on the hundred billion grey cells that – literally – have shifty, ruthless, self-serving minds of their own.' **The Times**

Can you trust your brain? You might feel justified in thinking that you know what your brain's up to, and that you're in control. Sorry. Think again.

Your brain is vainglorious. It deludes you. It is pigheaded, emotional and secretive. Oh, and it's also a bigot. This book reveals the fiendish little sins your brain gets up to behind your back.

Cordelia Fine's book tells you everything you always wanted to know about the brain – and plenty you probably didn't.

Paperback   UK £8.99
ISBN: 978-1840467-10-9